Manless: A Celebration of the Single Life and Achieving Deeper Fulfillment on Your Own

Debbie Danowski, Ph.D.

Manless

A Celebration of the Single Life and Achieving Deeper Fulfillment on Your Own

Urano
publishing

Argentina - Chile - Colombia - Spain
USA - Mexico - Peru - Uruguay

© 2024 by Urano Publishing, an imprint of Urano World USA, Inc

8871 SW 129th Terrace Miami FL 33176 USA

Urano
publishing

Cover art and design by Luis Tinoco

Cover copyright © Urano Publishing, an imprint of Urano World USA, Inc

The first edition of this book was published in May 2024

ISBN: 978-1-953027-36-8

E-ISBN: 978-1-953027-38-2

Printed in Colombia

Library of Cataloging-in-Publication Data

Danowski, Debbie

1. Personal Growth   2. Relationships

Manless: A Celebration of the Single Life and Achieving Deeper Fulfillment on Your Own

Dedication

This book is dedicated to my sister Karen who has always been there for me, before, during, and after my manless time. I have learned so much from you, and I love you very much.

Acknowledgments

Putting together a book is a team effort, both professionally and personally. I am blessed to have so many wonderful people on my team. This book would not be possible without my amazing agent Linda Konner whose belief in this project from the very beginning was unwavering. We have been together for many years now, and I am deeply grateful for her continued belief in me and my work. Best agent ever!

I am also so very grateful for my editor Lydia Stevens who from the beginning understood on a profound level the importance of this book for women everywhere. She truly embodies the essence of female empowerment. I am honored to be part of Urano World's inaugural English-language publishing efforts and grateful to everyone there who made this book a reality from the cover designer, Luis Tinoco. to the copy and production editors, Kerry Stapley and Derek McPhee. My gratitude extends to Urano's authors as well. To be working with so many distinguished authors with knowledge in such a wide variety of important topics is truly a gift. Thank you everyone!

I am also blessed to work at a university that values diversity, inclusion, acceptance, and most of all, kindness, in addition to academic achievement. I have been a faculty member at Sacred Heart University for over twenty-five years, and so many wonderful people have helped to make my time there one of professional and personal growth. This environment has given me deeper academic knowledge and personal insight. Thank you to everyone at SHU!

My work with the nonprofit Food Addiction Institute and the INFACT School reflects my deep commitment to food addiction recovery and has resulted in meeting, working with, and becoming friends with many wonderful and amazing people who share my commitment. Under the leadership of Esther Helga, this organization has flourished and brought attention to one of the world's most destructive addictions while at the same time providing me with an opportunity to fine-tune my writing and research skills. Keep up the good work FAI!

On a personal level, I am blessed to have so many wonderful and supportive friends in my life. I am grateful for each one of you and especially the support you give me in our weekly Zoom meetings. I could not have survived the pandemic lockdown without my dear friends. Thank you all so very much!

My family provides a solid foundation of love and strength in my life. My sister Karen and I have been through a lot together. I don't know where I'd be without her continuing support. Likewise, my niece Melissa and nephew Tony, along with their children are a great support and inspiration to me. I also gain strength from those no longer in my life—my parents, grandparents, and brother—who each played a role in bringing me to this point. I love you all so much!

The animals in my life bring me great joy and love. All my fur babies have touched my heart and I could not imagine my life without them. My love of horses began at H.O.R.S.E. of Connecticut during a time when my life had changed drastically. I remain grateful for Patty Wahlers and her army of volunteers who work so hard to rescue abused and neglected horses, and sometimes people too. I am also very grateful to 13 Hands Equine

Rescue for everything they do to save horses, including my two new babies. Keep up the good work everyone!

I was very happy over ten years into my manless life when I met Peter. I didn't want a relationship, and I certainly wasn't looking for one. Quite the opposite, I was happy with the life I had created and determined not to let anyone take it away. At the time, I didn't see how a relationship could add anything to the wonderful life I already had. I was wrong and continue to be proven so. Though our relationship is anything but traditional, it is a true gift and one that works better for me than I ever could have imagined. Thank you, Peter, for your love and support.

Finally, I am grateful to God for the life He has given me. There are no words to express my deep gratitude for the amazing gifts I have been given. My life today is a true miracle. Thank you God.

Table of Contents

Introduction

This book is not about hating men or man-bashing. If you are
looking for a book like that, you are in the wrong place. This
book is about one person and only one person. The person you've
neglected more than any other in your life. The one you've criticized more often and more harshly than anyone else. The one
you've worked hard to make "better." The person you've blamed
for everything that's gone wrong in your life and the one person
on the planet who you spend more time with than anyone else:
you.

In this book, you will not be reading about ways to attract a
man or make yourself a "better" partner. There will be no tips
about changing the way you look to please a man or finding ways
to "accidentally" get into a relationship. The only relationship
this book will discuss is the one you have with yourself, which is
the single most important in your life.

Within these pages, you will be encouraged to pay attention to
yourself where, and as, you are now. And though you will be encouraged to try new things, this book is based on the belief that
you are already "good" enough, if there is such a thing. It begins
with the idea that you are a worthy person just as you are. You do
not need to do one thing to prove your worthiness. You do not
need to have a certain hairstyle, income, position, or house to be

"acceptable." And, most of all, you do not need to have a husband or partner to be worthy of a fulfilling, happy life.

You are exactly where you need to be at this moment in time. Whether or not you are manless by choice, chance, or circumstance, your life is unfolding just as it is meant to for your highest good. The universe is working to make your life whole, complete, and perfect. And your manless life gives you the ideal opportunity to allow this to happen.

As a manless woman, you have time and space for personal growth and fulfillment unlike any that is possible in a relationship. You have the opportunity to focus on yourself, your likes and dislikes, and your goals and dreams. Your life truly is about you, and if you want, it can be about making a greater difference in the world.

At first, because of the many messages we get from society about the value of monogamous romantic relationships, your manless life may seem overwhelming, lonely, or even frightening. Or, if you've been manless for a while and are happy with your situation, you may feel as if society doesn't understand your happiness. Perhaps you are bombarded with offers from friends to fix you up or offered sympathy from those who believe being married is the only road to happiness.

Whatever your situation, this book is designed to remind you of who you are: an amazing, strong woman who is perfect exactly as she is. It is not necessary to have a man in your life to be complete and whole. You do not need a man to take care of you. Quite the opposite, your manless time is the beginning of an incredible journey of self-discovery and fulfillment unlike any you have known before.

Whether you have been manless for two minutes or two decades, and whether you need to be reminded that it's OK not to be in relationship, or are in a partnership struggling to find your sense of self outside of that relationship, you can make this a deeply inspiring time full of love, happiness, and fulfillment. Manlessness is a precious opportunity for growth beyond anything that you can imagine.

How do I know? I have lived this journey each and every step of the way. I was manless first by circumstances, and later by choice, for nearly ten years. I wouldn't trade one minute of that time for anything. Though I am currently in a relationship, I still practice the lessons and skills I learned during my manless time to maintain a strong sense of self, and I am eternally grateful for the gifts my manless time has given me. Because of my manless time, I no longer look to anyone else to make me happy. I took time to cultivate activities in my life that I would not give up simply because I am in a relationship.

Now, it's your turn. You deserve the best that life has to offer. And it's your job to take care of yourself, to make sure you are open to the gifts that come your way. Before getting into the specifics of how to do this, you'll first read about the attitudes present in society that sometimes get in the way of knowing how spectacular you are. It's important to understand where the ideas about equating happiness with romantic relationships comes from.

After that, you will learn about ways to celebrate your manless time, things you can do to deepen your satisfaction with your life, and reminders of things you may have forgotten. You'll also learn about the Ten Freedoms. If you've been manless for some time, then you are probably familiar with some of them, but you may not have ever put them all together in this way. There is little in society that encourages you, as a woman, to celebrate your manless life.

After that, you'll learn to explore your creativity and the grander plan of your life. Sometimes women in relationships ignore their spirituality simply because they do not allow themselves solitude. Manless women have a unique opportunity to engage in activities based solely on their inner spiritual longings.

Following that, we will discuss the idea of spirituality and community service. Making a difference in the lives of others fills a spiritual need for many women, manless or not, but those not in relationships have the time and energy to pursue these activities.

You'll learn about how to acknowledge the fears most women have about being manless. Even those who have been without a man for several years sometimes feel afraid. We'll also discuss the idea of facing everything and regrouping. You'll read about the deep fulfillment that comes from pets, either your own or visiting with someone else's, followed by ways to enhance your future and help other manless women gain the acceptance you have found.

It's time for the celebration to begin. Turn the page and let's go.

CHAPTER 1

You Are Perfect

I'm single because I was born that way.

—MAE WEST

You've seen them before. You know them almost the minute you meet. They are the married women who, upon learning of your manless status, immediately evoke their best sympathetic look and subtly shake their heads, as though you have a fatal illness. This is usually followed by repeated offers to send their husbands over if you ever need a handyman. Though they are mostly well-meaning, these sentiments aren't at all helpful to you personally or to society in general. They only add to the mistaken belief that manless women are to be pitied, that there's something wrong with them.

This couldn't be further from the truth. Manless women are courageous and strong, oftentimes going against societal expectations. Even more importantly, manless women know they have the ability to shape their lives, that each experience adds to the fullness of their already beautiful lives.

Rather than being offered sympathy, manless women need to be admired for having the strength and determination to forge their own paths, to be themselves, and to make choices that support their own needs. Being a manless woman is not about having something wrong. Instead, it is about celebrating the gifts in your life that are not possible when in a relationship. You have freedom and time to devote to yourself without worrying about your partner's needs. Your time is your own.

Even more than all of this, you know that it is up to you to make your life fulfilling and happy. You don't make the mistake of looking to others to meet your needs. You have learned that happiness is your responsibility and not something that is dished out by someone else on good days.

Years of Conditioning Are Wrong for Today's World

Manless women direct their own lives, learning each day how to make themselves happy. They know that though life can sometimes be challenging, there is a deep fulfilling happiness that comes from making choices that create enthusiasm. They are aware of the passion that is inspired in solitude and through creativity. And even more, they understand that spirituality, emotional growth, and self-awareness all involve the deep contemplation that only takes place when one is alone.

Despite all these benefits, there are many who believe that manless women need to be pitied because they are single. Through years of conditioning, many women have been brainwashed to believe that they must have a man in their lives to be successful, safe, and happy. For many, "snagging" a man to marry is the ultimate prize. And though things are changing, the transformation is slow in coming.

Manless women are often looked down on for either being selfish or unable to commit to a relationship. Sometimes they are told, either in words or overly dramatic sympathetic looks, that there is something wrong with them for not being in a relationship. Years of folklore about spinsters and old maids with too many cats have taken their toll on single women everywhere. Rather than feeling the pride of their accomplishments and the merits of their courage, single women sometimes feel ashamed or ostracized from a society that expects two-person households.

Occasionally, however, manless pride slips through the cracks and takes to task the "shoulds" that nearly drown all women. In a recent article in *Woman's Day* magazine, author Eleanore Wells ponders the issue, "What do you call a fascinating, charming, middle-aged woman who has never had a husband (or children)? There isn't a word to describe us."

These thoughts are important for several reasons. The first is that they were published by a magazine whose mission from its earliest days as a free-in-store A&P menu planner in 1931, focuses on catering to women who are married and have families. More than that, the article was published in the "Real Life" section of the magazine, which includes first-person essays about women's lives today. This suggests being single is a reality for a growing number of women.

Though publication of an article about single life is progress, it's still sandwiched between articles about protecting your family from household dangers and recipes to surprise your family. In other words, it's progress, but there is still so much farther to go in achieving acceptance for manless women. This acceptance begins with the women themselves. Like Eleanore Wells, manless women everywhere need to speak out and educate the world about the benefits of their choices: choices to earn their own money, travel to places they've always wanted to see, buy a home they love, and generally follow their dreams to create fulfilling lives.

Times Have Changed

The time has come for women everywhere to respect *all* the choices made by each other. There was a point in history when lesbian and gay relationships were considered "evil" or "wrong." Thankfully, as a country, we have come a great distance from this viewpoint. Now, it's time to do the same for manless women everywhere by recognizing that women of all sexual preferences can choose to be "relationshipless." It is no longer acceptable to offer sympathy for a lifestyle choice that has far too many benefits to even list here. It is no longer OK for women to believe they are incapable of leading fulfilling, happy lives without men. And most of all, it is downright disrespectful of manless women to insinuate in any way that there is something wrong with them.

Even more than that, it is factually incorrect. Because of their lack of marital relationships and society's misunderstanding about the benefits of their lifestyles, manless women have had to fight against traditional beliefs and institutions to gain even a small amount of the acceptance readily bestowed upon married women with children. In other words, manless women have had to be strong and fight their way through a maze of unacceptability. How on earth could someone, anyone, think there is something wrong with them?

Despite all of this, there are many who believe being without a man is tantamount to missing an appendage. A big part of this is idea is based on false notions that don't fit the realities of today's lifestyles. Our great-grandmothers' very survival depended on "latching" onto a good man who could provide for their needs. Women simply were led to believe they were not able to handle the physical demands of building shelter, farming land, and tending to herds of cattle without men to help. Therefore, it was important that women returned the favor by caring for their man in the form of cooking meals, cleaning house, and tending to the children. In other words, it took two people working together to survive.

Obviously, we have come a long way since these days. And yet, our attitudes are still firmly rooted in the past. They are carefully nurtured and passed down by our mothers and grand-mothers. It is from these attitudes that many women have decid-ed a manless existence may be harmful and dangerous. Today, however, women are no longer dependent on men to survive. Life, though still difficult at times, is not as physically challeng-ing as it once was. Houses are no longer built without the use of machinery, and it is no longer necessary to farm the land to have available food.

Sometimes it's easy to forget how quickly things have changed. It was only a little more than 150 or so years ago that most Amer-icans lived without running water and electricity. Water had to be hauled from wells and kerosene lamps were used to light a house. Wood was cut, split, and used in stoves for both cooking and heating. And it took the better part of a day to do a load of laun-dry. There were no dishwashers or refrigerators, and people grew most of the food they consumed. Daily life in early America was time consuming, and it took two people to manage the needs of a household.

Attitudes Are Slower to Change

Though things have changed a lot, attitudes haven't progressed as quickly. There are still a large majority of both men and women who believe that women are incapable of living alone and taking care of their own needs. This creates a troubling life for manless women since they are often looked down upon or treated as if they cannot manage their lives.

Though we have made great strides with technology and have wonderful advancements to simplify our daily lives, attitudes about women have been slow to adapt. In fact, some women still cling desperately to men as a means of ensuring their financial and physical safety. And, in some cases, the women are earning more money than the men they believe are keeping them safe.

How many times have you looked at one of your friends and wondered how she could possibly be with the man she has chosen to marry? Have you ever thought about why some women seem to always have a man in their lives? Or has it ever occurred to you that many, many people—both men and women—remain in unhappy marriages because the alternative is often overwhelming and frightening, as are the outdated attitudes of family and friends they would have to face during a divorce?

Also, consider the fact that our tax regulations provide bonuses for married couples and penalties for those filing singly. In addition, Americans are given tax credits for having children, and it is considered politically correct to be married. In the history of the United States, there has only been one president, James Buchanan, who remained a lifelong bachelor. All other presidents either came to office married or were married in office, and those married in office number only three,¾ John, Tyler, Grover Cleveland, and Woodrow Wilson.

All these things show exactly how ingrained the idea of marriage is in our society. And though this doesn't necessarily have to be a negative thing, it has turned into one for manless women. While there is nothing wrong with marriage in general, it should not be seen as the end-all, be-all for a woman's life, nor should single women be penalized in the form of higher taxes and negative attitudes.

Manless Women Need to Move Forward

As a country, it is time for us to move beyond these outdated attitudes. As individuals, it is time for us to offer encouragement and kindness to each other regardless of someone's marital status. Manless women should never be discriminated against nor mocked for their choices. And taking this a step further, they should not be pitied either.

While going against societal norms is almost always difficult, manless women have a special challenge since many of them tend to be isolated from other manless women. There are few special areas for manless women to meet or share their experiences. Even social media groups geared towards singles often turn into matchmaking sites. As a result, manless women often feel different and disconnected from society; there are so few role models for them to follow.

It is past time for all of this to change. Manless women everywhere need to stand tall and proud of what they have accomplished, whether that's creating an amazing career, doing meaningful volunteer work, buying their own home, or pursuing any other activity to improve their lives. Manless women have gone against what is considered "normal" in society, and that alone is an accomplishment. They have stood up and said, "I choose a different life than the one everyone else thinks I should have." And they have done this despite repeated, and sometimes, strong pressure from their mothers, grandmothers, fathers, siblings, friends, and coworkers.

Manless women have met the challenges, saying they want a lifestyle that works for them, not one that's based on centuries-old attitudes and religious beliefs. While a manless woman knows the benefits and happiness that are possible from a life free of a committed relationship, it is time for everyone else to realize and understand that being manless is a choice, not a disease nor condition requiring sympathy or explanation.

Being Manless Is a Gift

Being manless is a gift, and it needs to be treated as such, beginning with societal acceptance. In our society, being married or in a relationship is widely recognized and even promoted as being very special. If you doubt for one second that society holds marriage as something special to be celebrated, consider all the time, effort, and money that goes into planning and holding a wedding, the average cost of which is $30,000 in the United States.

As a manless woman, you may feel a certain guilty pleasure about your status, but it rarely, if ever, is treated by others, or perhaps even yourself, as the gift that it is. In the same way that marriages are celebrated, we also need to recognize the joy of the single life. We need to have the same excitement and joy for those choosing a manless life as we do for those who are married. Both are worthy of celebration. And both are fulfilling lifestyles that deserve acceptance.

Change in this area has been slow to come but progress is being made every day. And that progress is only possible if manless women are not afraid to speak out about the amazing lives they have. As Eleanore Wells did in the article she wrote for *Woman's Day*, it is time to let others know how wonderful a manless life can be.

Some women, especially those in unhappy marriages, find it hard to accept that a manless life can be fulfilling. Many of these women have chosen to stay with the men in their lives out of a belief that they are not able to make a life for themselves. Perhaps they have convinced themselves that they must remain in their marriages for the sake of their children. It's time to rethink these actions. Women are no longer dependent on men to survive. They don't need to stay in marriages or enter relationships that are not fulfilling, even for reasons of love. Women can now support themselves financially and emotionally.

Teach Our Daughters to Be Proud

Staying in unhappy marriages teaches our daughters that they must be dependent on men to survive. This sends the message that there is something wrong with them if they do not have men in their lives. Our society has many movements that encourage our daughters to be all that they can be and to choose any career path they want, but we still expect that they'll be married when they make these choices.

Though some progress has been made, it is not nearly enough to ensure that women of the future will understand all the choices available to them. To my knowledge, no large group of people has ever advocated that being manless can be happy and fulfilling. Instead, as politically correct as we have become, we have stifled voices of manless women since they do not fit with the normative expectations that have been passed down for several centuries. This stifling has come in the form of "incentives" and "expectations" such as tax breaks for those who are married, expectations of politicians to be married, and assumptions about two-person home ownership, none of which advance a manless lifestyle.

If you are reading this book to understand a manless woman in your life, whether it is your daughter, friend, sister, or coworker, I applaud you for being open-minded, and I urge you to keep that open mind as you read on.

Your Perfection

Now it's your turn. The purpose of this chapter is to help you recognize your perfection. Manless women are repeatedly told by society how "imperfect" their lives are, so rebuking this can be difficult. But it's not impossible with a little effort. To begin, let's consider your own attitudes about your single life. We do this not to judge, but simply to identify attitudes or behaviors that may not be serving you.

Take a few minutes to think about your life. How do you feel about being single? Do you consider it a gift or a curse? Are you lonely? Depressed? Joyful? Excited about life? Make a short list of five things you feel when you consider your single life, then take some time to reflect on what this list says about your current emotional state.

Remember, you are not judging your list nor your emotional state. You are simply noticing what you're feeling. Whatever you feel is OK. The point here is to pay attention to yourself and your feelings. We live in a society that encourages us to be in motion, and this keeps us distracted from ourselves and our feelings. The first step to caring for ourselves is to notice what we're thinking and feeling.

Looking at your list, consider what it would feel like to totally accept yourself and your feelings without having to run from or change them. If you feel sad, you can honor that feeling and take an action to express it. For example, you may snuggle under a warm blanket, cry, take a nap, write in a journal, watch a sad movie, or simply sit in a comfy chair and feel your sadness. It is not necessary for you to run from or change your feelings. Your feelings are perfect. You are exactly where you need to be at this time. By accepting your feelings, you will come to understand your own perfection.

Many times, we tell ourselves we shouldn't feel a certain way, or we should be stronger and better than our feelings. We try to force ourselves to overcome or get rid of feelings we have decided are wrong or bad. When we do this, we create an adversarial situation in our own minds, which results in us feeling badly about ourselves.

In other words, we use our feelings as weapons to beat ourselves up. We create an ideal image of how we think we should feel and behave. Usually, this image is based on the unrealistic pictures and representations we see in the media. In a television program or movie, difficult situations and complicated feelings are resolved in a few hours. This is not realistic. It takes however long it takes for us to experience our feelings and putting limits on how long a feeling should last only creates personal frustration. Accepting our feelings eliminates this struggle and simply enables us to pay attention to ourselves.

Imagine How Amazing It Would Be

By totally accepting our feelings, we would take away many of the negative ideas we have about ourselves and create an atmosphere in which we could learn to take care of ourselves. We would be able to acknowledge our feelings, take responsibility for them, then decide how we want to express them healthfully. For example, if we are angry, we may choose to pull weeds, go for a walk, lift weights, or write about our feelings. These are all healthy ways of expressing anger. If we are feeling sad or embarrassed about being manless, we could take a few minutes to write about our feelings, call a friend, or read something inspirational.

Yelling at someone, expecting someone to make our anger or sadness go away, or vindictively acting for retribution are unhealthy ways of expressing our anger or sadness and will only make us feel worse. Our anger is not a weapon to be used on other people or ourselves. It is a feeling to be acknowledged and expressed in a healthy way. The more we can accept and express our feelings, the healthier we become, and the better we will feel about ourselves.

As you go through your day, notice how many times you try to "correct" or "justify" your feelings. Do you tell yourself that you shouldn't feel this way? That you need to look on the bright side? That if you're too happy, no one will like you? That "good girls" don't get angry? Do you force yourself to think positively to hide other feelings? Are you using positive thinking to suppress some of your feelings? Do you tamper down excitement by telling yourself it won't last?

Once again, the purpose of these questions is not to judge or change anything. It's simply for you to notice what you're feeling. If we aren't aware of our feelings, it is impossible to understand who we are and what will make our lives fulfilling. Too many times, women are told they should or should not feel certain ways even though feeling is simply part of being human. By putting judgments or rules on how we should feel, we create unacceptance of ourselves and our lives. Not accepting ourselves can lead us to look outside of ourselves for happiness and satisfaction, which will ultimately result in frustration.

As a manless woman, it is important for you to accept and support yourself. While this is important for everyone, it is especially vital for those who are living lives outside of societally acceptable norms. Your strength will grow as you come to accept and honor who you are. You are perfect. You are exactly where you need to be at this moment to be able to move into the next moment and the one after that. Honor this moment by honoring your feelings.

Every time you start to judge or edit your feelings, simply say to yourself, "I love and accept myself and my feelings exactly as they are." When you find yourself thinking that you shouldn't be feeling something, simply acknowledge the feeling, then repeat that phrase. Imagine how powerful it will be when you truly do love and accept yourself and your feelings exactly as they are. Then, take a few minutes to feel grateful that you do not have to consider how your feelings may upset your partner. Instead, being manless gives you the freedom to focus solely on what you are feeling without worrying about what another person may be thinking. Keep reading to find out how you can not only accept your feelings but also celebrate your life!

CHAPTER 2

Celebrate Your Life!

The more you praise and celebrate your life, the more there is in life to celebrate.

—Oprah Winfrey

Life is a miracle. Your life is a miracle. Every moment you experience, every breath you take, every single day you wake up, these are all miracles. Though sometimes our lives may seem to be long, uphill battles, there is still magic in the fact that we are alive. Even if there are difficult things in our lives, there are almost always people, places, or things we can be grateful for and appreciate. While it's easy to take such positives for granted, it's important to notice and celebrate these parts of our lives. To start, think of three things (or people or places) that you enjoy having in your life; things which bring you happiness.

These things can be as simple as flowers outside your window, the warmth of a summer day, or a phone call from your best friend, or they can be as all-encompassing as your family, your career, or your lifestyle. It's important to pick things you genuinely appreciate in your life, *not* things you are told you "should" be grateful for or are lucky to have. Celebrating your life is about exactly that, celebrating those things in your life that you are happy with. The focus of this entire book is you, *not* what others think about you, your lifestyle, or the choices you make. That is one of the biggest benefits of being manless, you don't need to worry what your partner may be thinking about your likes and dislikes. If, as a grown woman, you love stuffed animals, then have them! In a manless life, there is no one there to make you feel self-conscious about whatever it is that makes you happy.

Some of the non-people-related things I celebrate in my own life include: my pets, being able to walk, my comfy bed, sunshine, my home, the Calm app, the ability to move easily without pain, my teddy bears, having a vehicle to drive, technology, my job, books, newspapers, birds, flowers, trees, home-grown vegetables, my research, and so many other things. Now, it's your turn to think about your own life to find three things you enjoy. If you are currently in a difficult or sad stage of your life, do your very best to put aside all that you believe is wrong with your life and, for a few minutes, think about three things that are working. These can be as simple as having tissues to wipe your tears, a pillow to rest your head, and a warm blanket to cover yourself.

Safe From Physical Harm

When I was newly divorced many years ago, the sadness I felt was overwhelming, and it lasted for many months. Nights, when I tried to fall asleep alone in my bed, were the hardest. After waking up most days feeling devastated, I realized I needed to find a way to go on and accept my new life as a single person. While I couldn't just wipe away my sadness (nor should I have tried to since they were part of my experience), I decided to begin thinking about one thing I was grateful for in my life as it was at that moment. At that point, the only thing I could come up with was a line from an old song that reminded me I was safe from physical harm. Even though there were many wonderful things in my life which deserved to be celebrated, I couldn't see them then.

As time went on and I kept reminding myself each night that I was grateful to be safe from physical harm, things began to improve. It was a starting point for me to recognize I could experience deep sadness yet still celebrate the life I had. I began to realize that my life was about more than the marriage I had lost. It was more than being part of a couple. And most of all, I started to understand that I deserved to be happy and celebrate my life whether I was in a relationship or not. Though these realizations took time, it all began with the simple act of appreciating one thing in my life. I truly believe that if I was able to do this then, you can also do it now. Begin where you are, and you will learn how to build on this as you continue reading.

Learn How to Celebrate

My guess is that there are a few, if not many, things in your life that are working but which you may not even notice. Take a few seconds to think about your job, your home, your friends, and your hobbies. Sometimes, we can get so focused on the one area of our lives we believe is not working that we forget about the other great parts of our lives. I'll give you ideas of things to celebrate and how you can celebrate them in the following pages. It's important to remember, though, that not everything I mention will work for every person. It's vital you only follow the suggestions which work for you. Do not force yourself to do something because you feel you "should" celebrate a particular area of your life.

For example, not everyone feels comfortable around, or gets along with, their family. For some people, staying away from family members might be a healthier choice. Others may find they have supportive and loving families. Neither situation is better. Please read that sentence again. Neither situation is better. Throughout the years, the idea of marriage and family has been romanticized as being superior to all other lifestyles. That is not the case, and this entire book is about breaking that stereotype.

While I do not suggest that having a family is a bad or negative lifestyle choice, I fully recognize that not all family situations are positive. It's time to put aside the idealized families many of us grew up watching on television or seeing in advertisements. Most families are not like those we regularly see in the media. Many families do not even resemble the images we've created in our own heads. Sometimes, when we see a family walking down the street or doing their grocery shopping, we think about how happy they look and how well they seem to get along. While this may be true in the exact second we see them, it's worth remembering that all families have problems, because all people, married or single, do. In other words, there is no perfect situation or family, and for many women, being manless is a much better situation than feeling unhappy in a relationship.

We are not out to demonize families or find problems within them. Doing so will only make us focus on other people and create problems where there may not be any. Instead, I am encouraging you to celebrate the parts of your life that are working right now, right here, today. If you're like I was after my divorce, then I encourage you to create a small-celebration foundation. For me it was "warm and safe and dry." If that works for you, you are welcome to use it. If it doesn't, then begin to think about what will work for you. Begin by thinking about ways to describe your life. Is your life exciting? Peaceful? Routine? Are you surrounded by nature or in a big city? Do you travel or are you a homebody? Are you social or quiet? Do you work hard or enjoy lots of leisure time?

Answering some of these questions can help you find a starting point much like my "warm and safe and dry" statement. If you are not able to come up with a word or two to use as a celebration foundation, then start by reading books, listening to songs, or even watching television to find words that will work for you. Some suggestions include strong, capable, loving, kind, gentle, serene, free, peaceful, exciting, innovative, smart, friendly, talented, creative, artistic, energetic, fun, bold, natural, grounded, spiritual, faithful, or trusting.

Even if this is the last thing you feel like doing right now, please do not skip over this exercise. I know personally how important it is. When I felt as if I had nothing else to hold onto in my life, I always came back to my celebration foundation words, "safe from harm" and they always made me feel better about my life. Even though there were other great things in my life, I couldn't see beyond these words. Having these words did begin to change that. After you've found your words, continue reading to find other areas of your life you may be able to celebrate.

A Healthy Body

Are you able to walk? Can you move about your day freely? Is it possible for you to participate in physical activities? Can you breathe easily? Are you able to remember most things you need to in your daily life? Do you have a sharp mind? Are you happy with the way your body feels? Can you see clearly? Are you able to hear? Do you feel textures? Is your sense of taste strong? Can you smell the things around you?

Though you may not be able to do all the things mentioned in the previous paragraph, focus on the ones you can do. If you can do all of them, it may be worth thinking about how fortunate you are. Right now, as you read this, someone is struggling to walk or breathe, basic things we take for granted. I do not write this to make you feel guilty, only to remind you of how amazing your body is. It can be easy to forget how important a healthy body is and even harder to think about celebrating our health. Unfortunately, many of us don't celebrate our healthy bodies until something goes wrong. I know this firsthand.

On February 12, 2011, as I sat at my kitchen table eating lunch, I was overcome with an overwhelming feeling of nausea. Every time I moved my head, I felt sick. I could not continue eating, and as I moved from my chair, I suffered severe motion sickness. When I moved, I vomited. I managed to stumble to a nearby sofa, yet laying down did not relieve the nausea. With each turn of my head, I was violently ill. It took days before I could move without experiencing motion sickness, and months before I was diagnosed with a cavernous angioma, a malformed blood vessel, that was bleeding in my brain.

On May 2, 2011, I underwent brain surgery to remove the cavernous angioma. Though I recovered well, for the next few months, even a slight movement of my head in the wrong way would create feelings of severe nausea. I was unable to look up while walking. I could not turn my head quickly nor could I look at someone while walking next to them. Some days, I would wake up feeling sick because I slept with my head in a certain position. There were entire days, sometimes several together, when I was unable to travel in a moving vehicle. My gait was off. Not only did I stumble a lot, but I also fell frequently. I was off balance, and quite often, I dropped things I was holding.

As the years went on, my health improved, and I was able to regain many of the things I had lost. A full recovery, however, was not possible because I had a veinous anomaly, what the brain surgeon called a "funny vein" that he could not remove because it is necessary to my ability to function. Today, though I am unable to travel and must limit my time in moving vehicles, I can walk. I still stumble and even fall sometimes, and I have had to move to a warmer climate to avoid winter's slippery ice, but the fact that I am able to take daily walks is a reason for me to celebrate. I also celebrate being able to move around in the world without experiencing the severe nausea I had so many years ago. I accept that sometimes I stumble, and that's OK. I've come to understand that if someone doesn't accept me for who I am today, they don't belong in my life. Because I learned this during my manless time, I can be fully myself in my relationship today without worrying if the way I walk bothers someone else.

I write all of this for two reasons. The first, and most relevant to this section, is to illustrate how important it is to celebrate a healthy body in whatever form that body takes for you. It never once occurred to me that I would or could experience brain surgery. It wasn't that I was ungrateful for my health. I honestly just didn't think about it much until I was forced to think about it all the time.

The second reason I write about my brain surgery experience is because I went through the brain surgery single. I was not in a romantic relationship. There was no man there to "take care of me," nor did I live with anyone other than my two cats. I did have, and continue to have, many wonderful family members and friends who helped me through this difficult time. For them, I am eternally grateful. But the bottom line here is that if I can survive brain surgery as a single person, I'm sure there are many things you, too, can survive and even excel in as a single woman.

Plan to celebrate your health. Choose one thing you are grateful for about your health. I usually begin with being grateful for my ability to walk. Throughout my life, walking in nature has helped me feel healthier and calmer. Looking at trees that are hundreds of years old and have survived strong winds put things into perspective. They remind me that I, too, am resilient and have survived many things. I also love looking at flowers. They remind me of the beauty in my life. Though your gratitude about your health may be different from mine, the idea is still the same, celebrate at least one aspect of your health. Begin by thinking about an activity you love, then figure out what part of your body allows you to participate in it. Think about how grateful you are for that part of your body. Remind yourself of this daily.

Mental Health

At first, the idea of celebrating your mental health may seem daunting, but it doesn't have to be. A celebration of mental health can be something as simple as listening to your instincts or expressing difficult feelings. As women, we have been taught for centuries to care for others yet have been offered little encouragement to express our own feelings or to care for ourselves. Many of us do not even know how to identify some of our feelings, and if we do, we don't quite know what to do about them.

As a first step, take a deep breath right now and observe what you are feeling. If you can't name what you are feeling, keep it simple. Stick to the four basic feeling words—glad, sad, mad, scared—and remember not to judge your feelings. Feelings just *are*. There are no "good" or "bad" feelings. Women have sometimes been taught that they "shouldn't" get angry or feel sad. This is not true. Everyone experiences these four feelings in their lives; sometimes we experience all four at once. When we judge our feelings, we put an added layer of distress in our lives that doesn't need to be there. So, simply observe what you are feeling and don't try to change it or make it go away.

This next step may be a little harder if you are used to judging your feelings and labeling them as "good" or "bad," but do your best to try it. Celebrate whatever you are feeling. If you're mad, celebrate the fact that you can notice and feel your anger. For some women who have never been allowed to express anger, giving attention to their feelings is a reason for celebration. If you're feeling sad, it's OK. There is a beginning and an end to every feeling. Sometimes they don't go away as quickly as we'd like or last as long as we'd like, so it's important to remember that they will come again, and you will survive.

For some women, feeling glad is even more difficult to celebrate than feeling sad or mad. Since, as women, we are taught to care for everyone else, when we feel happy, we may worry this will make someone else feel badly about their situation. One of the best things you can do for yourself is to erase this idea from your mind. You are not responsible for how someone else feels. Despite what you may have seen on television or been led to believe, you cannot control what anyone else feels. You can't even control what you feel. Your happiness does not take one thing away from someone else. It's OK for you to feel happy, and it's important for you to acknowledge and celebrate this.

Taking this a step further, it's OK for you to feel happy when you are single. Too often the media is filled with images of unhappy single women. Consider the crazy single cat woman trope. This image has survived for decades, whether it appear in an offhanded comment in a comic strip, a derogatory reference in a film, or an exaggerated character in a television show. The crazy, single cat woman mocks single women who have chosen to have pets, rather than men, in their lives. While the image is exaggerated for "comedic purpose," I find no value in mocking women who have made a choice to live a single life.

An important step in celebrating your mental health may be to rid your life of all derogatory images of single women. That comic strip about single women that your relative cut out and sent to you goes in the trash can. Those romance books that extol the virtues of married life need to be donated to the local library. The internet advertisements promoting dating services can be ignored, and the magazines telling you how to find the "perfect" partner can be recycled. Though you may see or hear some of these things through circumstances beyond your control, do your very best to surround yourself with positive images of happy, single women as a way of celebrating your mental health.

On a side note, if there is an area of your mental health that you feel strongly opposed to celebrating, it may be a good idea to look deeper into this. If you're feeling deeply depressed, severely unhappy with your body size, or extremely dissatisfied with your career, you may want to consider seeking professional help. Engaging a professional therapist can be a celebration of your mental health, especially if it motivates you to make changes to improve your life. Be sure to select a therapist with whom you feel comfortable. The goal here is not to make you feel badly about your life, but to encourage healthy growth.

Fun

It may seem repetitive to celebrate the fun in your life, however, it's important to notice and celebrate the things you enjoy. Take a few minutes now to think about at least one thing in your life that brings a smile to your face when you do it. For me, it would be spending time with my animals. Listening to one of my three cats purr when I pet them, watching my four bunnies playing with cardboard boxes, or walking with my two horses, all bring a smile to my face. I have fun when I spend time with my animals. I love to throw the ball down the hall and watch one of my cats run after it. It's great fun to see my bunnies up on their hind legs when I bring in a maple branch. Watching my horses run, bucking and rearing, around their paddock brightens my day. While these things are fun for me, they may not be for you. Each person is different and it's important to respect everyone's preferences, especially your own.

Many of us wouldn't dream of criticizing someone else's idea of fun, and yet the things we say to ourselves might be devastating. Some of us may not be able to identify things in our lives that feel fun. It may take some reflection to find fun things. Others may not have any fun things in their lives at present. Perhaps we've decided to wait until there's a man in our life before we allow ourselves to have fun. This is one of the biggest mistakes single women make—they wait for a man to provide them with entertainment. That's not the way it works. It is not possible for someone else to bring fun into your life. While you may have a fun experience with someone, the reason you like it is because you allowed yourself to have fun, *not* because someone else gave that sense of fun to you.

You, and you alone, are responsible for bringing fun into your life, no matter what that means to you. No one has the right to mock you for whatever you enjoy doing. Though you don't have to put pressure on yourself to create the perfect amount of entertainment in your life, it's worth being aware of which things in your life have the possibility to be fun. For example, is there a certain activity you feel drawn to but never allowed yourself to experience? If it's something you're not able to do right now, is there a way to bring part of it into your life? If you've always wanted to travel to Italy but you're not able to do that right now, can you visit the Italian section of a city or go to an authentic

Italian restaurant or museum? Allow yourself time to think about and create fun in your life. If you already have fun in your life, then celebrate it!

Friends and Family

For some, celebrating certain friends or family members is not possible, and that's OK. If there are people you are related to who have caused you great pain or harm, then it makes no sense at all to honor them. You may choose to simply avoid and ignore them. Not every section in this chapter is relevant to every person. You will need to pick and choose those areas of your life which you'd like to applaud; then forget about the rest. Please do be sure to celebrate at least one area of your life though.

If you are grateful for friends or family, then now is the time to celebrate their presence in your life. You may choose to do this by spending time with them. Schedule an outing for coffee, a shared trip to the library, a hike, or a shopping date. Whatever works for both of you is what you should do. Not only will this remind you of those in your life who support you, but it will also help you to remember that as a manless woman, you have free time to participate in activities of your choice without considering anyone else's schedule. It will also allow you to continue developing your skills in living a full life as a single woman.

If spending time with those friends and family members currently in your life is not possible, you may want to call, text, or connect on social media. Even taking a few minutes to look through a friend's online photos may help you to celebrate your friendship. A note of caution here: though most people look happy on social media, it's important to remember that these are single moments in time and not a summary of someone's life. Do not use these photos to make yourself feel badly. If that's the result, then skip right over this step. It is not designed to be used as a weapon against yourself, but instead, as an acknowledgement of your amazing life!

Pets

In addition to the people you'd like to celebrate, there may be furry friends you want to honor too. Though my life is, and has been, filled with many wonderful pets (all of whom deserve to be acknowledged), it was a three-month-old feral kitten who made me understand exactly how important pets are when embarking on a single life. Shortly before Tiger Lily came into my life, a relationship I was in ended. I was truly heartbroken and taken by surprise. I misunderstood the depth of the relationship which added to the pain I was feeling. In my sorrow, I instinctively knew that I needed to focus on something else yet was slightly hesitant to make a long-term commitment to caring for an animal.

I decided that if I were going to adopt a cat, it would not be a kitten, and it would not be feral, since I knew they had special needs that I may not be able to meet. As I was driving home one day, I saw a sign for a cat adoption event at a local pet store. I decided to go in and just look at the adoptable cats. It turned out to be a feral-cat adoption, but I was already on my way in, so I continued. The first cat I saw was a beautiful older black cat named Grace. I decided with a name like Grace, she was probably the one for me. I reached in to pet her, and Grace bit me, not in a hard vicious way, but still, a bite. I was far too emotionally fragile to even consider adopting a cat who would bite me, so I carefully moved onto the next cage to look at other cats.

As I peeked into various other cages at beautiful older cats, I couldn't help but notice a woman who was carrying a very small tan-and-black tiger-striped kitten on her shoulder. The kitten was purring loudly. I felt jealous that this woman had found the right pet for her as I continued looking through cage doors, not really being drawn to any of the cats I saw. In my fragile state, I was sure that none of the cats would want to come home with me, so I decided to leave.

Just as I turned toward the door, the organizer of the adoption event came up to speak with me. I mentioned how happy I was that the little tiger kitten had found someone to adopt her, and she explained to me that the woman holding her was a volunteer of the organization. She told me the kitten's name was Tiger Lily and they had found her living on the city streets only three weeks prior, yet she was available for adoption. The first time I held Tiger Lily, she began to purr loudly, snuggling up to me. I knew that despite the rules I had created about my dream cat, Tiger Lily and I were going to be a team.

Tiger Lily is now fifteen years old and she and I have been a team for almost that long. In our years together, we have welcomed twenty other animals into our home, moved three times, went on two vacations, and spent countless hours snuggling together. She came into my life at a time when I was totally devasted and has continued to be the focal point of my life with her unconditionally loving presence. If that doesn't deserve celebration, then I don't know what does!

Hobbies and Talents

Another important area of your life to honor are your hobbies and special talents. Before you skip over this section thinking you don't have any talents or hobbies that deserve to be acknowledged, take a few minutes to consider things which you may be taking for granted. For example, are you great at arranging flowers? Can you do a puzzle well? Are you a great bowler? Do you have a talent for yoga? Can you paint or draw well? Is traveling something that makes you feel alive? Are you interested in watching birds or camping? Biking? Swimming? Hiking? Running? Meditating? Knitting? Sewing? Cooking? Gardening? Reading? Embroidery? Making jewelry or candles? Playing an instrument? Photography? Coloring? Scrapbooking? Journaling? Singing? Decorating?

Any of these pursuits deserve to be applauded. It can be easy to overlook something we may have been doing for many years since it has been a big part of our lives. Or perhaps we've been so busy taking care of other people that we have neglected to have interests outside of our family or professional lives. That's OK up to this point; however, now that you have chosen to live a manless life, you will need to become more aware of your talents and the hobbies you have. In other words, it's time to pay attention to yourself. You deserve to honor those activities which are important to you.

A good starting place for either celebrating or finding a hobby may be to think about the interests you had as a child. Was there one activity or subject in school which always interested you? One that you couldn't wait for. Did one of your teachers complement a project or assignment you did? Were you known in school for being the one to go to for help with a certain subject? Did friends and family members ask your help with specific projects? Were you the one people counted on for knowledge in a certain area? Or was there an activity, place, or area which always made you feel happy and serene?

It may be helpful to write for a few minutes about moments in your childhood which stand out to you as being important.

Remember, it doesn't matter if the event was important to other people. This is about you and what you thought of it. For me, it was coming in second place in a poetry contest in fourth grade. Though I can't even remember what the poem was about, I do know that I cut out the small announcement in the local newspaper and kept it for many years. This was a clue indicating how important writing is, and would become, in my life. In addition to having published five books, I wrote over one hundred local newspaper and magazine articles, taught writing at the college level, and journal regularly. This book is a testament to my ability to pay attention to and honor an activity which is important to me.

Please understand, it's not necessary for you to have success in the activity or hobby for you to celebrate it. I use the writing example as one in which I am successful, but there are other activities I love and am not at all accomplished in. I have always loved painting and drawing. I truly admire people who can create visual works of art. Despite trying to paint and draw over the course of several years, I simply do not have the talent and sometimes end up frustrated by my inability to create anything close to a work of art. Still, I honor my interest in painting and drawing in several different ways: I realize that I don't need to be perfect to paint or draw if that's what I really want to do. If I have trouble believing this, then I choose a similar and less demanding activity—I grab a coloring book and color. I also take my celebration online by using a design program (canva.com) to put together social media posts or create images for my websites (debbiedanowski.com, nakomafarm.org) or I grab my camera and take pictures.

Though society tells us we must be successful to celebrate, we don't have to fall into that trap. Simply having an interest in an activity or hobby is reason enough to applaud yourself. If you already have a hobby or talent that's well developed, perhaps you can delve deeper into a new technique. If you have yet to discover an interest, consider finding a hobby right now. Give yourself permission to try and fail at many different types of activities or hobbies. Don't expect to be perfect, and above all else, do not pressure yourself in any way to compete with anyone else.

The act of finding and nurturing a hobby or talent needs to be celebrated. Celebration is defined as *the marking of an achievement by participating in an enjoyable activity.* In this case, the enjoyable activity is whatever hobby or activity you participate in while the marking of an achievement is the fact that you have made time to focus on yourself. Though this may not seem like much of an accomplishment, consider for a few minutes the ways women have been treated historically.

According to an article by Juliet Gardner on the *History Today* website, though women had earned the right to vote since 1929, they were unequal in mostly all other areas and considered "submissive and inferior" beings. She points out that "Many teachers and parents had narrow expectations for girls whose destiny was [...] marriage [and] a home and a family, with work just an interim measure between leaving school and walking down the aisle, rather than a career." She further notes that only 1.2 percent of women went to college during the 1950s.

Why should something that happened almost seventy-five years ago matter to you today? Consider the age of your parents and grandparents. My guess is that one of these generations grew up or were adults during the 1950s, thereby passing down outdated ideas and inferior ways of behaving to you. I've seen this a lot with the women I talk to and even in my own life. My mother was a teenager in the 1950s, and she was told by her parents to find a man to support her so she would always be taken care of. Though my father insisted that both my sister and I earn college degrees, he was not happy when my mother went off to work. This was not lost on my sister nor me. We were told one thing, yet observed quite a different one. Though both of us learned how to celebrate things in our lives and take care of ourselves, it did not come naturally to either of us.

Ironically, it takes some work for us to notice and celebrate any aspect of our lives, but it's especially challenging to notice those involving our personal talents and interests. As women, the idea of putting others' needs first has been ingrained in us for centuries and even passed down through the female members of our families. Now is the time for you to change this. Notice who you are. Pay attention to what you like to do. Understand how important you are in your own life. Vow to be the most important person in your own life, and act like it. You are worth the time and effort it takes to celebrate yourself, your life, and your gifts.

Work

Working in a job you love is cause for great celebration. Many people go off to work each day dreading it. If you are someone who has a job you enjoy, take time to celebrate. There are several ways you can do this. One of the best and most effective ways is to continue to work successfully at the tasks you are given. Whether you are in education, hospitality, the creative arts, cleaning, landscaping, transportation, or any other area, give your best every day to your job to celebrate your gratitude for having a job you love.

It's important to remember that the job you have may not be right for anyone else. Living a manless life is about taking charge of your own life and expressing who you are through that life. It is not about living up to other people's expectations. If you are happy with your job, then celebrate it!

A word of caution here. It's easy to get caught up in work while neglecting other areas of your life. This is not the purpose or intent of honoring your work. Having a well-rounded life is important and necessary for fulfillment. If one area has taken over your life, you may feel overwhelmed and stressed. This is not a healthy way to live, nor should you put yourself through so much stress. A manless life is about taking care of yourself and living the full life you have created by choice. Though work is an important part of our lives, it cannot, nor should it be, our entire life. This is especially true if you are working a job you don't like or are working two jobs to make ends meet. If this is the case, perhaps taking some time to think about what your perfect job would be is a way to honor the manless life you are creating. To be truly happy, there need to be other parts to your life than work. Realizing that can be a way to applaud the efforts you are making in the work area.

Yourself

Though you will read about celebrating yourself in the next chapter, it's worth mentioning here to remember how amazing you are. It's easy to get caught up in the expectations society and others have for you, and for you to feel badly about yourself when you don't think you're living up to what you "should" be doing. Yet, it's worth considering if what you "should" be doing is what you really want to do. While many years of societal conditioning may have led you to believe the only way to be happy is to be in a relationship, that's simply not true. There are plenty of women who are much happier living manless lives than they ever were when they were married.

As evidence, consider the divorce rate, which hovers around 50 percent, give or take a few percentage points. If everyone who was married had such a great life, then the divorce rate would be in the single digits. Instead, approximately half of all couples who get married later divorce. I know from personal experience that it's easy to think everyone else is happier because they are in relationships. This statistic tells a different story. Half of all couples who choose to commit to each other for life are so unhappy that they legally end their marriages.

As you continue reading, please try to remember this statistic. The reason I ask this of you is to keep you realistic so you don't fall prey to a fantasy world where "they lived happily ever after." Though it may be fun to watch a romantic comedy or read a romance novel, it is unhealthy to compare real life to the situations in those works of fiction. Keep in mind, they are just that—works of fiction—and as such, they are not reality. In fact, the reality of romance is similar to that of being manless; both take effort to achieve happiness.

Another thing to consider are the ways in which many women sacrifice themselves to be in a relationship. I'm sure we all know at least one woman who makes choices about her life depending on whether her husband will "let" her do what she wants or not. Just the other day, I was speaking with a woman as I was out for a morning walk. She told me her husband didn't like her to walk "down here," so far away from their house, so she walks in her driveway. While it's possible there are underlying medical conditions which make it safer for this woman to stay closer to her house, it is also possible that she has chosen to sacrifice something she really likes to do for the sake of peace in her marriage.

Sadly, there are women all over the world who make much larger sacrifices to be in a relationship. It's not uncommon for women to give up careers, houses, pets, hobbies, friends, and even family members to please their partners. While all relationships involve compromise, it is not healthy for a woman to give up something that is important to her so that she is able to remain in a relationship. In a true partnership, both people support each other's goals and wants. And as a manless woman, you can do and have anything in your life without worrying about pleasing anyone but yourself.

I am certain there are women in relationships who envy you for the freedom you have. I've spoken to far too many women for me to ignore the fact that many who are in relationships stay for practical, rather than romantic, reasons. I've known women who are so terrified to be on their own that they put up with insults and abuse, not realizing how lonely that kind of relationship is. I've also known women who stay married so that they don't have to support themselves financially. And I've known women who are 100 percent capable of taking care of themselves, yet they've convinced themselves they need a man to take care of them.

Of course, there are many women who are happily married and in healthy relationships. The point here is not to bash men or marriage. Both are like anything else: there are some good and some not so good. But the images we see in the media do not reflect the realities of day-to-day living. This is true of the images we see in life as well. How many times have you gone to an event, seen couples together, envied their happiness, and considered just how amazing their lives must be? Exactly how long did you see this couple and on what precisely were you basing your assumptions?

A Special Note About Holidays

Though this chapter is about celebrating the things you love about your life, there are times when you may want to celebrate special occasions or holidays with someone else. For some manless women, holidays can be stressful in ways that may not be apparent to others. Images of happy families and couples surround us. Stories of holiday magic and romance fill the airwaves with one channel devoting over a month to holiday romance movies. And while there is nothing wrong with any of this, manless women may find themselves buying into all the hype and feeling lonely.

Or perhaps these ideas are reinforced at the events you attend. If you have decided to attend one of these gatherings, the best thing you can do is to prepare yourself for comments about your marital status. Rather than feeling defensive, take the attitude of an explorer trying to understand why your marital status is a concern for the people who are asking you. Ask them questions when they make comments. Say something like, "Why do you ask?" or "Why are you concerned about whether or not I am married (or dating)?" Be sure to keep a calm tone of voice, like a report asking questions. You do not need to explain or justify your lifestyle to anyone at all.

Chances are good that if you are experiencing your first manless holiday, you may feel some loneliness. Of course, this depends on the circumstances in your life. If you are recently widowed or divorced, you may be missing your partner and you have my deepest condolences. Please know that the single kindest thing you can do for yourself during this time is to be gentle, loving, and accepting of your feelings. There is no need to go out and prove how together you are by forcing yourself to have a good time. You do not need to make others feel better, and you most certainly do not have to attend any function which you don't want to be at.

This holiday, and all others, should be about how you want to celebrate and not what others expect of you. You may choose to ignore the holiday completely or celebrate by yourself. Watch a special holiday-themed movie. Spend extra time with your pets. Cook a special meal. Take a long, hot bath or indulge in a special gourmet treat. Volunteer your time, or take a long walk. However you decide to spend holidays, understand the images you see in the media are inaccurate. No one, whether they are single or married, has a perfect holiday all the time. Many people feel stress and anxiety when they spend time with their families. Some people envy those who spend the holidays alone.

Remembering these things will help you to avoid the pity trail where you believe everyone else is happy but you. Pitying yourself serves absolutely no purpose. It only makes you feel more miserable about something that may not even be true. Your happiness is your responsibility. Finding a man will not solve all your problems, and it may even create more problems, especially if you've chosen him out of desperation rather than love. If you want a happy life, it's up to you to make a life that's happy.

Starting from where you are now, you can create a manless life that you love. Then, should you decide to enter a relationship, you will do so out of choice rather than desperation or to meet societal expectations. And if you decide to remain manless, then you will have created an amazing life filled with love and passion of your own making. So, read on, and understand exactly how precious you are!

CHAPTER 3

You Are Precious!

You have been criticizing yourself for years, and it hasn't worked. Try approving of yourself and see what happens.

—LOUISE HAY

You are a miracle. How does it feel when you read that? My guess is that you've come up with a long list of reasons why you are not at all miraculous. Maybe you've even started to think about all the things you consider to be "wrong" with you. Or perhaps you're replaying old tapes from your childhood or from a relationship that ended badly. If you're doing any of these things, do your best to try and stop right now! This way of thinking is not helpful. It goes directly against the amazing life you are working to create. Even more than that, your negative self-talk is untrue. The very fact that you are breathing is a miracle. Let's use that as a starting point—you are alive, and life is a miracle. Consider how amazing your body is to keep you breathing and alive.

Building on this, you, personally are also miraculous. There never has been, nor will there ever be, another person exactly like you. Think about your finger for a second, specifically your fingerprint. No one else in the world has the same fingerprint as you. Your fingerprint is used for identifying your uniqueness throughout the entire world. Not even your relatives have the exact same fingerprint as you. No one else has all the same experiences or emotions as you, either. Even if you have siblings or are a twin, your experiences, feelings, thoughts, and emotions are solely your own and make up the unique and precious being you are. In the same way, your manless life is an individual creation, made from your unique choices.

Small Hands

Sometimes when we read things like this, it makes us feel uncomfortable, especially when we may be feeling badly about ourselves for not being in a relationship like we believe we "should" be. Take a second to consider how much power you are giving your marital status. Sure, maybe you went through a lot when your last relationship ended, or perhaps you've felt alone for your entire life. Though you may be overwhelmed by this, the fact is, this is only one part of your life, not your entire life. More importantly, to define yourself by this one portion of your existence when so many other things about you are miraculous, doesn't serve you and makes little sense.

Consider someone who has small hands. Though this person may not like her small hands and it may bother her that she is unable to do everything she wants to, her small hands do not completely define her existence. They are simply a fact of her life, not something that deserves judgment as "good" or "bad." Instead, this person can simply think of her small hands as a part of her life. If she is under a certain age, then perhaps her hands will grow, or maybe they will stay the same size. Either way, there are many other aspects of her life she can choose to focus on.

Try to think of your manless life in the same way. It is simply a fact. There is no need to pass judgment on it. It is one part of a life that you are in the process of making amazing and wonderful. If you're like many women, you have used your marital status to define the "goodness" of your life. Meaning that if you are in a relationship, then your life is good, and you are worthwhile. And if you're not in a relationship, then there is something wrong with your life and therefore with you. The single most important thing you can do for yourself is to stop judging your relationship status. As Louise Hay notes in the quote at the beginning of this chapter, criticizing yourself doesn't work. It never has, and I don't believe it ever will.

Cheerleading For You

Yes, we've all heard about tough love and making improvements from critical feedback, but when we're talking about your relationship with yourself, it's much different. As you probably already know, there are some people in the world who are all too willing to offer unsolicited criticism or opinions about your life. It's easy to find something wrong with someone else's life. It takes very little effort to criticize someone, and many people judge others to make themselves feel superior. While you can't change these people, you can work to become your own biggest cheerleader.

Many people are very quick to complement friends or family members. They treat them with care and consideration. Yet, when it comes to themselves, they turn into judgmental shrews who constantly say mean things, telling themselves they're not good enough without being in a relationship, or that they are unlovable because they are single. If even a little of this rings true with you, it's important to become aware of the things you are saying to yourself and how often you are criticizing yourself. Though it may feel natural to call yourself a slob when you spill sauce on your new shirt, think about whether you bring this self-talk into everything you do. Are you unhappy with yourself all the time? Do you constantly think negative thoughts about yourself? Can you never seem to do anything right in your own eyes?

If you've answered "yes" to even one of the above questions, I would strongly urge you to try to stop doing these things. Criticizing and judging yourself serves no purpose in your life. And many times, when we have a difficult relationship with ourselves, this carries over into all aspects of our lives. I don't know of any woman who ever experienced happiness in her life or chose a healthy, loving relationship of any kind while she was critical and judgmental of herself. Quite the opposite, most women who are abusive towards themselves choose men who act the same way towards them. It's what they expect, since that's how they treat themselves.

To have a happy, productive, manless life, you'll need to turn into your own biggest cheerleader. There's no negotiation about this. Do not skip this step because you think it's stupid. Instead, embrace the idea that you can love and encourage yourself in the ways you think a relationship will. It's your job to take care of yourself and to cheer yourself on. You deserve to acknowledge, and even celebrate, yourself.

Begin at the Beginning

To begin cheerleading for yourself, you'll first need to become aware of what you are saying to yourself. Make it a point to notice your thoughts throughout the day. For example, when you wake up, is your first thought about how awful you look that day? Or do you avoid looking in the mirror at yourself because you think you're ugly? As you move through your day, do you criticize the way you do things or doubt your ability to handle certain aspects of your life? Do you spend time thinking about how inadequate and stupid you are? Or are your thoughts more subtle, telling you that you can't do certain things because you're not strong enough, brave enough, or smart enough?

Once you're aware of your thoughts, the next step is to refuse to give them any power, and this means *any* kind of power—negative or positive. Instead of trying to argue with your thoughts, which many of us have done, simply notice them. Let them float through your mind as if they were clouds, nothing more and nothing less. When you see a cloud in the sky, you don't argue with it. You don't question its existence, and you certainly don't label it wrong or bad. It's the same with the negative thoughts that come into our minds. Simply notice them, and let them float away, giving them as little attention as possible.

If you try to "correct" your negative thoughts about not being loveable without a relationship, then you are giving them power and putting energy into them. If you simply notice them as a fact of life and let them float away, they eventually lose any power they may have had over you. Giving awareness to them also takes away their power. If you try hard not to think about the negative thought that just came into your mind, you are still giving those thoughts energy, and that takes up space in your head.

Please understand that this is a process, a long-haul way of living, and not something you will be perfect at the first time you try it. Though we live in an instant-gratification world, there are things that take time, and this is one of them. Changing a lifetime's worth of beliefs and attitudes does not happen overnight, nor should you expect to be perfect, or even good at a new way of thinking, in the beginning. This process is about taking small steps each day, trying out what works for you, and adapting lifestyle changes as you move through your days.

Many of us have come to believe that if we can't make an enormous change overnight, the change will never happen. Not only is this idea a reflection of our "quick and easy" societal values, but it is a setup for labeling ourselves as failures when things don't turn around immediately. This label gives us permission to stop trying. Rather than putting so much pressure on yourself, give yourself the love and gentleness you deserve. Allow yourself time to try new things, develop new habits, and change your attitudes. Do not pressure or bully yourself into making changes. Gently welcome new attitudes into your life. Slowly make small changes and cheer yourself on as you witness little improvements in your life. There is no race and no need to be the "best" at any of this. The idea, here, is to allow yourself to see how amazing you are and how comfortable you can be in your life, because you don't need to be in a relationship to make yourself happy.

Nothing Grows Without Water

As you move through this process of using affirmations and making changes in your life, you may experience periods of sadness. Sometimes it may seem as if this sadness comes from nowhere in particular. It may not make sense or be consistent with the circumstances of your life. However, it's important to notice this sadness and to understand where it may be coming from. Many of us have ignored ourselves for so long that when we do pay attention to who we are, there is a period of mourning for all the times we didn't acknowledge ourselves in the past.

I don't think I will ever forget the first time I looked in a mirror, into my eyes, and said out loud, "I love you." Tears welled up, and I began to sob a deep, primal sob that shook my entire body. I had to sit down and let it all pass through me before I could go on with my day. I was completely shocked by my own reaction. I understood, on some level, that I wasn't always considerate of my feelings and needs, but this sobbing was beyond anything I ever expected. I came to understand that this was my soul, some call it their inner child, experiencing a deep sadness for being ignored for such a long time. I had rarely ever expressed positive feelings toward myself before, and when I did, the pain of forsaking myself for so long washed over me.

As time went on and I continued to do this, the tears disappeared. They were replaced by a deep love and appreciation for myself, one that cannot be had from anyone else, and is absolutely necessary for a truly authentic, amazing life. When I talked about this experience with someone else, she said, "Nothing grows without water," meaning that I needed the tears to experience the joy I now feel. Just as plants and trees need water to grow and show their magnificence, so do people.

Though tears may be part of your process, they do not have to be your entire experience, nor is it a good idea to dwell on them. Instead, treat them, too, like clouds floating by. The tears will come, and they will go. There's no need to make your experience more painful by adding judgment to them. Simply understand that tears are part of life and part of the growth process. And remember that though progress may feel painful, you will survive the tears and move into another phase of your life. You are an amazing woman who deserves to give herself the attention she wants and needs. There is no one else who can do this for you. This is your life, and it's up to you to make it wonderful. So, if you need to, shed your tears for the sadness you may feel about being manless, then keep growing!

Affirmations

While I'm sure you've heard about affirmations before (and you may even be using them already), let's take a second look from a manless perspective. Why would you take time out of your life to use affirmations? What would be the point? Take a second to consider how nice it feels when someone compliments you. Do you feel warm inside? Or do you cringe and tell yourself that they're just being nice? Do you make excuses for whatever they complimented, saying that it's an old shirt or you bought the shoes on sale? Or do you smile and graciously accept the compliment simply thanking them?

The way you deal with a compliment reveals a lot about you. If you say something derogatory or counteract the compliment, then you are giving it back. If you simply express gratitude, then you have learned to appreciate yourself. It is my hope that you will come to appreciate your awesomeness and simply thank the person who has complimented you.

In a manless life, we take responsibility for bringing goodness into our lives. We understand that being in a relationship does not automatically make us feel good about ourselves. One way to begin feeling good is to give yourself compliments in the form of affirmations. These affirmations do not have to be intricate or complicated. They can be simple statements reflecting how you feel, or want to feel, about yourself. The important thing is to keep them in the present tense so they don't become unreachable. While you know best which affirmations will work for you, I've included a list below of some that have helped me through the years. Though the list is long, choose only one or two to work on in the beginning. Do not overwhelm yourself with trying to use every affirmation on the list. Some may not be right for you, while others fit well.

Affirmations to Consider

I love myself.

I am healthy.

I am happy.

I am beautiful.

I am capable.

I am strong.

I deserve to be happy.

My life is filled with love.

I am successful.

I am confident.

I am getting better and better every day in every way.

I am powerful.

I am likeable.

I am loveable.

I love and accept myself exactly as I am.

I am worthy.

I am at peace.

Of course, there are many, many other affirmations that you can use, but this list is a good starting point. Read over each affirmation and choose the one that feels most uncomfortable. This is probably the area in your life which you need the most help with. If it feels too uncomfortable, then begin with one that seems less threatening and return to the other one at another time. Each morning when you wake up, look in the mirror, directly into your eyes, and speak the affirmation you've chosen. Then, as you move through your day, keep your affirmation handy, perhaps writing it down and putting it on the fridge or in your office where you can see it regularly. Simply say the words and let whatever feelings come up float away like clouds.

Keep at it each day and don't try to make charts or measure your progress. Just say the words as often as you are able to, and forget about the rest. You don't have to reach a goal or make drastic changes in your life. Simply say your affirmation day after day. Some days, you will feel better after saying it. Some days, you will feel worse. And some days, you will not feel at all different from saying your affirmation. Just trust that things are happening inside of you, and don't try to record your progress or reach a goal. Just keep saying your affirmation.

I used the affirmation, "I am capable," for many months without noticing any difference in my life. Many times, I felt ineffective, and yet I continued saying these words. One day, several months after I began using my affirmation, I was in an airport. My plane was delayed, and I needed to make sure I ate certain foods due to a medical condition. I had expected to be in an area by a grocery store where I would be able to purchase these foods. As I began to panic, one thought rose in my mind, "I am capable." I didn't purposely think about my affirmation, it just appeared when I needed it. That very thought allowed me to take a second look at what foods were available in the airport, and I was able to get what I needed. To me, this is a testament to how subtly affirmations do their work. It is my belief that if I can experience this, you can, too.

Expectations

This chapter, and even this book, would not be complete without a discussion about expectations. Expectations—those of ourselves, those of others, and those from others—can be insidious and cause great misery in our lives. When we expect things to be only one way, we have closed the door on other possibilities. This is especially true where our manless life is concerned. If we expected that we would be married or engaged at a certain point in our lives, then the life we have now may cause us to feel as if we've failed. We may even believe that it's not possible for us to be happy unless our expectations are met. This is not true.

There are many times in our lives when it's better that our expectations go unmet. Think about that man you may have expected to marry or the career you expected to have. Did it work out? Did it make you happy? Think about where you are right now in your life. There's a good chance that you expected to either be married or in a long-term committed relationship at this point in your life. The fact that you are reading this book means your relationship either didn't work out or isn't going as you expected. Right now, you are at a turning point. You have the power to turn your life around, to take steps, and to make improvements without expectations about how it will turn out.

When you have expectations about anything, especially if they are high or unrealistic, you are blinded to other gifts that may come along in your life. The career you expected to be boring may turn out to be your greatest passion. That book you thought was stupid might just help you to change your life. The party you expected to be dull could be the very event where you meet one of your dearest friends. The hobby you thought you would hate could be the start of a brand-new pastime.

The point here, is to keep your expectations and your judgments to a minimum as you work through the process of living a manless life. There are times when you will feel uncomfortable and even grumpy about the things in your new life. That's OK. Expecting everything to be quick, easy, and happy is not only unrealistic, but also a setup for you to fail, which would give you permission to quit. Our minds can be very tricky. Sometimes they create situations to make us stay where we are. Change can be scary, and minds work to protect us from fear. Our minds can thwart change by looking for things to criticize or by finding reasons for why something we're trying won't work. The easiest way to sabotage our efforts is to have unrealistic expectations. Then, if the expectations aren't met, we have the excuse we need to quit.

Do not fall for this. You are too smart to believe these things. While a few of the activities in this book may not work for you, there are many that will. Everyone is different, yet there are some universal truths for all human beings, one of which is the idea that we are responsible for making our lives full and happy. Our happiness is our job. Expecting anyone else to make our lives good will only result in disappointment, as it is not possible for someone else to "fix" our lives or create happiness for us.

Too Good to Be True

In line with this, it's important to recognize outside influences that may affect the way you treat yourself. Specifically, think about the images you see in the media. Even if you are aware of their falseness, you are surrounded by them, which makes it nearly impossible to remain uninfluenced by them. For example, as an Associate Professor of Communication Studies, I research food advertisements to understand the unhealthy behaviors portrayed in these ads. I am 100 percent aware of the marketing techniques used to make us want to not only eat the food advertised, but to overeat it. I am also intimately aware of the photography techniques used to make foods look appetizing, and the emotional appeals designed to convince us that eating certain foods will make us happy. Yet, there are still times when I see a food advertisement and am drawn into believing the unrealistic promises advertised.

Take this example about food advertisements and think about the same thing with the too-good-to-be-true relationships portrayed in the media. From as far back as the 1950s when television first became available to mass audiences, we have been conditioned to believe that having love, romance, and family members in our lives is the only way to be truly happy. Though these things may bring some of us happiness, they also bring many of us great pain and grief.

The point here is to first be aware of the images we surround ourselves with. We have a choice about what we watch and read. We do not have to allow these outdated ideas into our consciousness. Then, the next step is to challenge these images in our own minds. Think about what you see on television, then remember the reality of the current divorce statistics. I'm not suggesting that you develop a critical attitude about relationships, only a realistic one. Not all relationships are wonderful or bring happiness to those in them. Not everyone who is committed to a man is happy or feels loved. And, most of all, not all families are safe, healthy, and nurturing.

So, when you begin to feel expectations and judgments moving in, do the same thing you did with negative thoughts—acknowledge them, then watch them float away like clouds. Do not spend time chastising yourself for having expectations or judgments. Simply accept that this is part of human nature. You are not bad or wrong. You are simply human, and that's OK. What you do after that is up to you and will determine the quality of your life. Watch them float away and move yourself forward, or give them power and quit. As always, the choice is yours. Choose wisely.

CHAPTER 4

The Ten Freedoms

Some people say I have attitude—maybe I do... but I think you have to. You have to believe in yourself when no one else does—that makes you a winner right there.

—Venus Williams

As a manless woman, you have a freedom that is seldom experienced by married women. Unfortunately, rather than celebrating these freedoms, single women oftentimes allow society's attitudes about marriage to erase the possibilities these freedoms bring. Many women take little, if any, time to consciously consider their lives once they are in relationships. Many times, the relationship itself becomes the goal. The woman may think incessantly about whether or not he is ready to commit, get married, or have children. When there is no romantic relationship, finding one almost immediately turns into a pursuit. Rather than creating goals based on inner preferences, many single women seek relationships to distract themselves from taking responsibility for their own lives.

Being a manless woman means that you take full responsibility for your life and your happiness. While this can seem overwhelming at times, it also offers a freedom which is not possible while in a relationship. Being manless means you can plan your life based on your needs rather than the needs of both people in the relationship, thereby avoiding costly personal compromises.

While you may be envying married women, I can all but guarantee that some are also envying you. While our society is very quick to idealize romance and marriage, it is equally as swift to ignore the compromises and treatment women often receive in these relationships. This book is about independence from these outdated ideas and celebration of the possibilities manless living affords.

In the following sections, you will find a discussion of the ten freedoms manless women have. As you read, please be sure to savor each freedom and consider how it manifests itself in your life. In some cases, not all the freedoms will apply to you. If, for example, you have small children who are still in school, you may choose to live and work near where they attend classes. Of course, this is a choice that only you can make, yet it's important to recognize that a freedom is available to you, even if you decide not to experience that particular freedom. Read on and discover how free you are!

Freedom #1: The Freedom to Live Where You Want

A woman I know spent much of her adult life following her husband around from one military base to another as he progressed in rank. She had never once decided where she and her family would live.

Someone else I know had a husband who wasn't in the military, but he worked for a company with offices in several states. Each time he was needed in a different office, she moved her family. She, too, never made a choice about the place she and her family lived.

These two women do exist, and their situations are real. Maybe you even know someone in a similar situation. Though these women have done nothing wrong by moving with their husbands and families, they do not have the same kind of freedom a manless woman has. Manless women can choose where they want to live. Of course, there may be considerations beyond personal preference, such as employment possibilities, but the choice is still dictated only by the woman making it. Where she lives is not the result of the person she is married to.

Even if you are 100 percent positive that you want to live where you do right now, take a few minutes to think about where you dream of going. Would you like to live near the ocean? By a lake? In a city? Near a desert? By a river? In the woods? On a mountain? In the US? In another country? Warm weather? Cold weather? Sunny? Rainy? Metropolitan? Rural? Large house? Cabin? Cottage? Historical house? Farmhouse? High-rise? Studio? Condo? Artist colony?

Take a few minutes to consider the possibilities. Is there somewhere you've always wanted to live? A place you know of that feels like home? A home in a certain style? If you are unable to change your living situation at this time, this exercise may seem useless, but it's not. Thinking about where and how you'd like to live not only allows you to appreciate the freedom you have, but it also helps you to be in touch with your own dreams and desires. In other words, it's an important step in getting to know yourself, which can sometimes be a life-long process.

If you are planning to move or considering it, take some time to really think about where you want to live. Rather than settling for the easiest or most convenient place to live, think about where you really want to live. Look online at different house styles. Research and visit different towns or cities you are considering. Join social media groups devoted to the places you dream about. Look online for local newspapers and travel centers. Visit open houses in your dream area. During this time, it's important to look at as many possibilities as you can to help you make your decision.

If you're used to depending on others to tell you where and how to live, this will be a big step in your process because it will ask you to consider your decisions based on your desires, rather than the needs of others. If you're accustomed to living where you want and maybe even already live in the home of your dreams, then take a few minutes to check in with yourself to make sure the home you have still works for you.

When I was forty-four years old, I moved into my dream house—a log cabin on twenty-eight acres in Northern Connecticut. The two-story cabin was beautiful. It had tall ceilings and large windows that overlooked a beaver pond. It was on a quiet portion of a dirt road and had a woodstove that provided toasty heat. The stairs to my bedroom were made of halved logs and the cabin was positioned on a hill with a curving dirt driveway. There were trails in the woods, and eventually I created an area with two run-in sheds for horses. It truly was my dream house, and I loved living there for twelve years.

As I grew older and my balance issues from the brain surgery worsened, my dream house turned out to be too big of a challenge for me. Carrying wood up to the woodstove was difficult. The uneven ground proved to be too much of a challenge and resulted in me falling many times. The ice and snow in the colder months often created a dangerous situation bringing me to the realization that I needed to make a change.

As I write this, I now live in a one-story house in a warmer area with flatter land. I love my new home; it is also, now, my dream home. The point here is that it's OK to have a new or changing dream, and it's vital you make choices based on where you are now. Work to meet your needs at this point in your life and when your needs change, adjust. Do the best you can to acknowledge where and how you'd like to live. And most of all, understand that you have been given a gift as a manless woman; you get to decide exactly where you would like to live.

Freedom #2: The Freedom to Work Where You Want

When you are part of a couple, your choices about where to work can be limited by a company's proximity to your mate's job, income levels required to support certain lifestyles, and expectations about the type of job that's "acceptable" for women such as teaching or nursing. As a manless woman, you can work where you want and in the type of job that feels right for you. You don't need to think about working close to your partner's job or making enough money to keep a joint household running. You don't have to consider anyone else's views about what is acceptable for you to do. Being manless means being free to pursue your dream job, the one you may never have told anyone about. It means discovering what type of job you want to work and figuring out how to make that happen. It may mean making drastic choices to support your dreams, or it can be something as simple as requesting a transfer from your current employer.

The point here is that no one can or should dictate where you work. It is your right to choose your own career. Even if you're certain you won't be able to support yourself with your chosen career, you still have the opportunity and time to take small steps to bring this type of work into your life. For example, if you've always wanted to be an actress but are unwilling to earn lower wages while waiting for your big break, perhaps you can get involved in community theater productions, or maybe you can go back to school to teach high school drama, or perhaps you can take an acting course. Most of these things may be done while still working at your current job.

If you are new to the manless life, take some time to think about what you've always wanted to do. Put away any voices in your head that tell you your career goals are not possible, or that you're too young or too old. Instead of listening to them, figure out a way to make your aspirations happen. Perhaps you can begin slowly by going to your local library and checking out a book about your chosen career. Or maybe you can set up an appointment with someone who is doing the work you're interested in. You may even be able to join a social media group where you can contact others working in your chosen profession. Perhaps you can serve as a volunteer to try out your new career. There are many ways to begin a new career, and as a manless woman, you are free to try any and all of them.

Many women, even those who have been manless for years, have never given their careers much thought. They may have settled into a job because it was convenient, or because that line of work was expected of them by their family members so they never considered alternatives. If you're unsure of what kind of career you want, there are many interest and personality tests available that can help guide you towards those careers that suit you and that you're most likely to find satisfying. You can find these tests by conducting your own search online, or by contacting a local college, university, or career coach. You are worth the time and effort it takes to find a career you love. Not only will working at a career you love improve the quality of your life, but it will also make work seem more like play.

I stumbled into my career quite accidentally, based on a smell. When I walked into the halls of a state university to interview for a position as a program assistant, I could smell the slightly woodsy aroma of hundreds of books that filled professors' offices. To me, that was the best smell in the world. I got the job and worked as a program assistant for several years, and while there were many things I liked about the job, most notably the college environment, I knew inside it was not yet my dream position. A few months later, I saw an ad for adjunct faculty members in the English Department at the University where I had completed my undergraduate degree. I applied and was granted an interview. Then, I didn't hear back for a year. Finally, twelve months later, I was asked to teach two introductory writing courses.

I learned as much as I could about teaching and came to discover that I loved interacting with the students and teaching them to write. After a few semesters of teaching as an adjunct professor, I went back to school to earn my PhD so I could qualify to teach full time. I began a career that I still love to this day, twenty-five years later. Though it took time and great effort, I can honestly say it was worth it. I am still filled with love for my job, and I'm grateful to now be part of the Communication Studies Department where I teach advertising and public relations classes in addition to journalism courses. The time it took to find and earn this position pales in comparison to how many hours I have enjoyed my work throughout the past twenty-five years.

There is a deep joy in discovering and working at a career you love. As a manless woman, you do not have to concern yourself with the expectations of a partner. You are truly free to discover and work at the job of your dreams. Who knows where that will lead you? The excitement of giving birth to a new career can be part of your manless journey, and it's a true freedom for you to enjoy.

Freedom #3: The Freedom to Control Your Environment

Do you like loud music? Soft music? No music? What about the temperature of your living space? Do you prefer coolness or great warmth? Is there a favorite color you want to paint the walls of your bedroom? Do you like flannel sheets on your bed? Is there a special coffee maker you need in your kitchen? Do you want to fill your living space with flowers? Plants? Pets? Are you partial to hardwood floors instead of carpeting? Do you like fluffy pink towels or bunny slippers? If you work at home, do you require intense quiet time for long periods? Do you like to have the windows open even on a cold winter night or a hot summer day?

As a manless woman, you have control over your living environment. You do not need to consider whether your partner is too hot or too cold, likes or dislikes certain types of sheets, or is allergic to pet dander. You get to choose not only where you live, but also the conditions of your environment. One of the most productive and nurturing things a manless woman can do for herself is to set up a living space that reflects her preferences. Living in a home with things you love not only feels good, but also makes you feel loved and cared for.

Much of this book is about paying attention to yourself and taking action to make your life more pleasant for you. A good place to begin is with your living environment. Once you've decided what type of living space you'd like, the next step is to create a welcoming environment. Keep in mind that what's welcoming to you may not be so for anyone else. This is only about you. If you live with children or a roommate, you may need to take their personal spaces into consideration, but if you can't control all areas of your home environment, be sure to have an area that is only yours where you can create a nurturing space.

Though you may be tempted to skip over this exercise, please don't. A nurturing space is one of the greatest gifts you can give yourself. Even though it's easy to make excuses about not having enough time or money to make changes to your living space, do not fall into that trap. You don't have to reserve days or weeks to make your space nurturing. Start small, and build up momentum. If you love yellow, find one small yellow item you can place in your room a vase, candle, pillow, or flowers. It doesn't have to cost a lot. It simply needs to give voice to your preference for a certain color.

Once you've added one item you like to your living space, make a point of looking at it over the next few days. How does it make you feel? Do you like it? Is it truly an item you like, or does it reflect someone else's idea of what you "should" like? Do you feel embarrassed, ashamed, or even unworthy that you spent money on something seemingly so frivolous? Or are you proud of yourself for paying attention to your preferences? Even if you're not quite sure how you feel about this item, consider how you feel when you look at it. Are your feelings nurturing and positive? Neutral? Or something else? The important thing is to notice what you're feeling, then take a few minutes to understand where these feelings come from. For example, if you feel unworthy or embarrassed about spending money on yourself, try to think about where that feeling comes from. Did you receive messages when you were younger about not being important? Were you told that you shouldn't spend money on yourself or have items you love? If so, consider taking small steps to change that mindset by reminding yourself that you are worthy of having things that you love in your life.

Once you notice what you're feeling, you can take steps to support yourself. If you've inadvertently chosen an item that you absolutely hate, then it doesn't make sense to keep it in your living space. You'll need to try and find another item that will feel nurturing. If you absolutely love the item you've chosen, use this as information to place a similar one in another part of your living space. During this process, it's vital that you are patient with yourself. It's OK to try several different things before settling on one that fits. There is no right or wrong here, and it may take many tries to know how you're feeling.

Many women were never taught to pay attention to their feelings, nor to discover their own likes and dislikes. This process of discovery is a gift of a manless life. You have the freedom to create an environment you love to spend time in, and to learn what things go into that environment.

Freedom #4: The Freedom to Become Your Own Best Friend

You've heard it before, I'm sure. *Be your own best friend.* Yet what, exactly, does this mean? And why does it matter? It's actually quite simple. The goal here is to treat yourself the way you would treat your very best friend. Think about this for a second. Would you say to your best friend the things you say to yourself? Would you treat her as you do yourself? Take a few minutes to ponder these questions. Many of us were told to marry our best friends, however, putting your happiness in someone else's hands is a sure way to create misery. No matter how wonderful another person may be, they can't be everything you need. No one can. It's just not possible. Being your own best friend provides you with someone you can always count on, who will always be there for you in exactly the way you need her to be.

Most of us would never speak to our best friend the way we speak to ourselves. Many of us would not ignore our best friend's feelings and needs the way we often do to ourselves. In fact, many of us would say the exact opposite words to our best friends that we say to ourselves. In general, we are kinder to other people than we are to ourselves. Yet, throughout our lifetime, we will spend more time with ourselves than we will with anyone else. Even if we look at this from a practical perspective, consider how damaging it is to repeatedly say negative things to yourself. Not only are you damaging your self-esteem, but you have also set up an adversarial relationship with yourself. This requires you to continually try to change yourself.

During your manless time, you can begin to love and accept yourself as your best friend. In addition to using affirmations, you can, as you move through your day, start to notice the way you treat yourself. Do you often ignore your physical needs and wait until the last possible second to grab a sweater when you feel cold? Do you eat lunch when you feel hungry? Do you work hard to ignore your feelings? If you feel happy, do you reprimand yourself by saying the happiness won't last? Do you criticize yourself for being sad and needing a few minutes to gather yourself? If someone treats you poorly, do you make excuses for them while ignoring the hurt you feel?

Becoming aware of how you currently treat yourself is the key to becoming your own best friend. Once you're aware of the negative ways you treat yourself, you can begin to change those habits. Work first towards stopping the negative habits, then move into doing nice things for yourself. Though it will take time and effort, the payoff for learning to care for yourself is great. You will no longer feel the need to criticize yourself. Instead, you will treat yourself with love and kindness, in a nurturing, caring way. To be filled with love for yourself will provide you with the chance to make loving choices in your life. This will enhance the quality of your life and allow you to feel happier and more content.

Think about how wonderful it feels to spend time with someone you love, whether it's a friend or your child. You feel more positive and generally better just for having spent time with that person. These same feelings can come from being your own best friend. And the best part is that you do not have to look outside yourself to another person to feel love. The love will come from within you, which is something no one can ever take away. Though women who are in relationships can also become their own best friends, manless women have a greater ability to do so, since they do not have the distraction of a relationship to take attention away from themselves.

Freedom #5: The Freedom to Make Your Own Health a Priority

Many women who are in relationships spend a great deal of time focusing on their partner's wellbeing while ignoring their own. Instead of making an appointment for themselves to have a physical, they send their partner. Rather than taking time to exercise, they encourage their partner to do so, even watching the children so he can go to the gym. As a manless woman, you can focus on making your health a priority without the distraction of a partner. You can do all the things that make up a healthy life such as eating right, exercising, getting enough sleep, and managing your emotions.

Eating healthy, nourishing foods will not only make your body feel better, but it will also result in greater health. If you enjoy cooking, set aside time to look at healthy recipes and shop for the ingredients. Don't be afraid to experiment with different spices and healthy ways of preparing food. You may want to consider preparing food in advance to have healthy food choices during the week. Make a big batch of steamed vegetables or soup to avoid last-minute unhealthy food choices. If you've never cooked and don't feel comfortable experimenting, you may want to consider signing up for a healthy cooking class. You can usually find these in your area by going online and looking for adult enrichment courses.

Exercising is another important way to make your health a priority. Before you skip over this section, know that I'm not advocating spending countless hours in the gym on a treadmill or any other machine. There is nothing wrong with these machines and if they work for you, go for it, but I firmly believe exercise can, and should, be enjoyable. At the very least, it can be tolerable. Think about the activities you used to do as a child. Did you love to ride your bicycle? Was playing tennis your idea of fun? Did you like golf or basketball? Maybe you bowled or roller skated. Did you like to ride horses or hike in the woods? Whatever you enjoyed doing, if you are physically able, why not give it a try again? If you're not physically able, then think about something else that may interest you. This can be as simple as taking a twenty-minute walk around the block each day.

Making sure you get enough sleep is also an important part of taking care of your health. It's easy to get caught up in whatever you are doing and neglect sleep. Unfortunately, consistent lack of sleep can lead to health problems in the future. As a manless woman, you get to decide what time you will go to sleep at night and what time you will wake up in the morning, without having to consider a partner's lifestyle. When planning your sleep time, as with everything else in your life, be sure to take into consideration your personal preferences. If you prefer to stay up late at night, do your best to schedule a later morning so you can reserve at least seven hours for sleep. If you're an early riser, then be sure you go to bed at least seven hours before you plan to wake up.

Learning to manage your emotions is another important part of your healthy lifestyle. There are several ways to do this, but some of the more well-known methods are meditation and journal writing. Even if you've tried either or both in the past, it's worth trying them again. A good way to begin meditating is to look online for free meditation sessions, or, if it's in your budget, you may want to use a meditation app such as the Calm app. Meditation and journal writing can work well together. Journal writing is as simple as sitting down and writing about what you're feeling. Meditation helps you to observe and release these feelings. Both meditation and journal writing are effective in helping to ease anxiety and stress, making them wonderful options to support a healthy lifestyle.

Freedom #6: The freedom to Trust Yourself

So many women ignore their own needs and lack trust in themselves and their abilities. Historically, women have been taught to "listen" to their husbands and to trust their husband's advice above their own. This idea reflects patriarchal societies and has been passed down through generations the same way the idea of "landing a man" to feel secure has been. Consider, for a second, the logic of trusting someone else to know your needs better than you do. Now, take this a step further and think about the fact that this man could be compromised in some way that makes his decision-making skills less acute.

In this scenario, not only have you chosen to listen to someone else's advice about what is best for you, but you've also taken advice from someone imperfect (as we all are), who may not be the healthiest of people. For instance, consider a woman who takes the advice of the man she is married to. She is so accustomed to him that she may not realize he has a unique perspective, one that doesn't reflect the best thinking on the given subject. She may not even understand how deeply wrong his advice is. Likewise, consider taking advice from a friend rather than listening to your own instincts. What if that friend is somewhat jealous of you? How helpful do you think her advice is going to be?

As a manless woman, you have the freedom to learn to trust yourself and make choices based on this trust. This protects you from the whiplash of listening to other people each time they comment on your decisions. Though it can take effort to learn to trust yourself, it is a skill that will change your life. Consider how amazing it would be to make decisions based on your own self-knowledge rather than asking others what you should do. While it's OK to speak with others and ask their advice, in the end, the healthiest decisions about your life come from you, not anyone else.

During your manless time, you can develop this self-trust. Though there are many ways to begin trusting yourself, a good first step is to begin listening to yourself. Grab that sweater when you feel cold. Have a drink of water when you feel thirsty. As you begin to listen to and honor your physical needs, you will become more practiced at hearing and managing your emotional needs. If, for example, you're feeling tired, perhaps you can schedule a nap or some time to rest. If you're also feeling sad, writing about it, or calling a friend to understand where the sadness is coming from, will help you to "flex" your self-trust muscles. This self-knowledge will eventually become routine and will allow you to make decisions based on your own preferences.

Freedom #7: The Freedom to Be Your Own Motivation

As you're reading this, I'm sure you've noticed a common theme of listening to yourself. This idea directly counteracts hundreds of years of opposing practices governing women, which is why it builds the foundation for a manless life, one that is based on your own choices and is fulfilling happy regardless of your relationship status. The freedom to be your own motivation is the culmination of many of other freedoms. When you are your own motivation, your life becomes an amazing experience!

Women who live in the modern world may take this freedom for granted, but it is my belief that most women, even those who are single, don't live their lives according to their own motivations. Many times, women subtly give away their power. They might cancel plans to accommodate others or neglect their own preferences to attend events with family members. Whether in a romantic relationship, with their children, in a friendship, or with their parents, many women are masters at putting the needs of others above their own. Most women have not been encouraged to live their lives based on their desires, but are instead taught to take care of others.

Being your own motivation may be a foreign concept to you, and it can be scary and filled with negative messages about being selfish. Though some of these messages may have come from our families, the media is filled with images of selfless mothers and wives who are applauded for ignoring their own needs. Think for a few seconds about the television programs and movies you've watched, or even a recent ad you've seen. Likely, women are depicted in nurturing, "mothering" roles. Of course, today's media is somewhat different than that of years ago. But there is still a consistent thread running through it of nurturing, selfless women. Though these programs may be entertaining, you do not need to buy into their concepts of nurturing women putting aside their needs for others.

In a manless life, your needs are important. The things you'd like to achieve in your life matter. The activities you participate in should come from your own desires, not anyone else's. If you're not sure what you like to do or how you want to spend your time, it's worth finding out. It's important to listen to yourself. Think about the reactions you have to things. Perhaps look at various activities online or in magazines. Go to the library and pay attention to the kinds of books you are drawn to. Start in the nonfiction section and walk up and down the aisles reading the titles. Is there a book about an activity you've always wanted to try?

Woodworking? Knitting? Home repair? Gardening? Whatever it is, find a book that calls to you and look through it. If it appeals to you, take steps to either find out more information or begin doing this activity. If you are not interested, try another and another until you find something that you like.

At first, you may feel uncomfortable, even criticizing yourself for taking so long to figure out what you like to do. Do your best to stop the negative self-talk. This is not a race. No one is judging you. There is no time limit to getting to know your likes and dislikes. It's likely a lifelong endeavor, and you are worth the effort. Do not pressure yourself into making hasty decisions or giving up. Give yourself the same time and attention you would give to anyone else in your life. Be kind and considerate with yourself while you learn more about things that interest you.

As you move through this process, it's possible you may feel some initial sadness in the same way you did when you began using affirmations. It's OK to feel sad. Do it anyway. Do not let these feelings stop you. Instead, move forward in self-discovery. Learn about your likes and dislikes so that you will have the freedom to be your own motivation.

Freedom #8: The Freedom to Make Your Mental Health a Priority

Is there something you're doing that is causing problems in your life? Are you spending too much money? Drinking too much? Missing too many days at work? Isolating yourself from friends and family? Overeating? Gambling? Feeling too depressed to get out of bed? Using sex to make meaningful connections? Meddling in other peoples' lives? Some of these things are a part of life and we can do any or all of them to some extent. The issue is when they begin to cause problems in our own life.

If, for example, you're avoiding social functions to have more time to shop, drink, overeat, or gamble, it's possible you may have an addiction. Or, perhaps these behaviors are keeping you from living a fulfilling life. Anyone who spends much of her day focused on certain substances or activities such as shopping, drinking, overeating, or gambling could be taking the joy out of the day and may need to consider getting help to manage this behavior.

It's no secret that COVID changed our world and our lives. Even now, there are still consequences from this period, some of which are specific to manless women, who may have developed a greater fear of being alone. Many lost loved ones, became depressed, or turned to substances to make themselves feel better. And while much has been written about COVID depression, there are many who are still unknowingly suffering the effects of the pandemic. If you haven't quite felt right, or if you've developed a behavior that is concerning you, as a manless woman, you have the time, space, and permission to make your mental health a priority.

While addiction and depression are serious mental health issues, many women suffer from general malaise, what used to be labeled as *melancholy*, without ever thinking to address the feeling. Sometimes making your mental health a priority is as simple as making time to nurture yourself with a hot bath or a nap. Other times, it will involve engaging a professional therapist or a Twelve-Step group. Whatever works for you is what matters. Taking time to contact professionals or do some online research can go a long way in helping you to understand what's going on in your life.

Remember, your manless time is about you, and making your life the best possible one you can. Making your mental health a priority is an important part of this.

Freedom #9: The Freedom to Develop More Meaningful Relationships

Being manless means you also have more time to devote to relationships with friends and family. Many times, women who are in relationships spend time only with their partners or children, pushing aside friendships and even family relationships. Unfortunately, these women miss out on the variety of deep connections which are so necessary to a fulfilling and happy life. And if the romantic relationship doesn't work out, they are often left feeling lonely and daunted by the task of cultivating new friendships. It's all too easy for them to convince themselves that they are too busy to spend time with friends or family members, thus leaving their lives solely focused on the relationship.

Humans are not meant to live in isolation; they crave connections of all kinds. The degree to which we need connection is an individual preference, but we all need people in our lives we can talk to, confide in, share experiences with, and feel supported by in difficult times. Perhaps, as you've entered your manless life, you've been blessed with wonderful friends and family members who have supported you. If so, it's important to give time to honoring these important connections rather than taking them for granted. Or, if you're like I was when I first got divorced, you need to rebuild some of these relationships and find new friendships. Neither situation is better than the other. Wherever you're starting from, the fact remains that deep meaningful relationships make our lives more fulfilling and help us to deal with difficult times.

The freedom to spend time developing meaningful relationships is one of the greatest benefits of a manless life. If you are beginning from scratch or if you feel as if the people in your life don't understand the person you've become, then perhaps it's time to begin searching for new friendships. While there are many ways to meet people, such as volunteering, participating in an activity, taking a class, or joining a group, it's important for you to discover a way that works for you. The first step is for you to get to know yourself well enough that you can create friendships with people you have something in common with. In other words, don't just randomly volunteer somewhere to say you did it. Take some time to discover the activities you like to do, and research possibilities in that area.

It's important not to fall into the "I-don't-need-anyone-else" trap. Oftentimes, as women, we try to live the "superwoman" ideal we've seen in the media. This dangerous ideal tells us that we can do everything and don't need anyone. This couldn't be further from the truth. If you are a human being, then connection is an important part of having a fulfilling, happy life. You're not weak, nor should you feel ashamed, for wanting friends in your life or for needing human connections. Being manless is not about isolating yourself from the world. Quite the opposite, it is about going out into the world and living an amazing, happy life filled with love of all kinds.

Freedom #10: The Freedom to Follow Your Dreams

All the other freedoms have led you to this most important one, the freedom to follow your dreams, your innermost longings, those things you may not even admit to wanting. This is your time to discover what these things are, and to make plans to do the things you've always wanted to do but have previously denied yourself. Now is the time to do some research, plan, and take steps forward. You are manless, and you have the freedom to do the thing you've always wanted to. Perhaps, at this time, you're not even aware of what that thing is, but as you begin to pay attention to yourself, your dreams will become clearer. You may even discover something you didn't know you wanted. Self-discovery is one of the joys of being manless.

As you consider following your dreams, be sure to listen to yourself. After years of ignoring our needs, it's easy to minimize our dreams, or to talk ourselves out of them by telling ourselves that we're too old, too young, too busy, or "too" anything else. Instead, think about ways to support yourself in making your dreams happen. Be flexible in the way these dreams are expressed. If you've always wanted to be an opera singer yet suffer from severe stage fright, perhaps you can take a first step of finding an opera singer who offers private voice lessons. Even if you don't enjoy the lesson, you've taken a first step, and that's what matters. You can, then, try another option. Make contact with someone in the field to arrange a tour of an opera house. Let yourself walk through the place and feel inspired. Perhaps you'll discover your real talent shines most happily backstage.

Put as much effort into making your own dreams come true as you possibly can. Be creative and think of ways to support your dreams. As a teenager, I was passionate about writing, yet never believed that I could become a writer. During that time, I sent a fan letter to a famous author asking her if she had any advice for me. Months later, I received a reply in which she encouraged me to keep writing. That single response meant so much to me. I never forgot it, and I did keep writing. Several years later, I took steps to meet other people in the writing community, such as a reporter for a local paper. Then, after two years in college, I got up enough courage to take a writing class and was invited by the professor to work for the school newspaper. Eventually, I published five books and wrote over a hundred articles for local newspapers and magazines. I can't know if any of this would have happened without that writer's initial response. Yet in my heart, I do believe each event, including that response, was a step in me following my dreams.

You, too, can take steps to make your dreams come true. Take a few minutes to think about a dream or two you have or have had. Do not judge this dream. Simply think about it, and listen to yourself. You are worth the time and effort it takes to follow your dreams. The first step is to listen to yourself to find out what your dreams are. You can do this!

CHAPTER 5

It's All About You

I gave up my struggle with perfection a long time ago.
That is a concept I don't find very interesting anymore.
Everyone just wants to look good in the photographs.
I think that is where some of the pressure comes from.
Be happy. Be yourself, the day is about a lot more.

—ANNE HATHAWAY

You've seen them on television, magazine covers, online, and in advertisements: the "perfect women" who always look beautiful and seem to have great lives. They have a certain look, including thin bodies, white teeth, dramatic eye makeup, large lips, long, polished nails; and impeccable clothing. They're labeled "beautiful" and made famous based on the way they look. And though things have expanded a bit, most of these women continue to have similar features and characteristics which reflect current societal ideals of beauty. In this arena, there is little room for uniqueness or quirkiness. Instead, conformity is the rule.

This conformity asks women to accept without question someone else's ideas about not only how we should live our lives, but also how we should look while doing it. We are all unique, and it's important to allow ourselves the freedom to create what's in our hearts. For some women, this can be making a clay pot, taking photographs of nature, making jewelry, decorating a room, knitting a sweater, or cooking a meal. For others, this might be designing a thank you card, writing a book, painting a picture, playing the piano, coloring, drawing, or scrapbooking. Still others may choose to express their creativity by playing chess, making keychains, rearranging furniture, daydreaming, or putting together a puzzle.

Whatever your idea of creativity is, as a manless woman, you can discover and nurture it. You can spend time in solitude engaging yourself in creative activity. You don't have to conform.

Perhaps you're someone who believes that creativity isn't important or that you don't need it in your life. Maybe you appreciate facts, figures, and science more than being creative. Or perhaps you've tried to pursue creative activities in the past to no avail. In other words, why should you care about being creative, and why on Earth is an entire chapter of this book devoted to it? Continue reading to find out the benefits of creativity.

Creativity Can Improve Your Health

Consider a benchmark study done nearly two decades ago in which researchers divided thirty-seven HIV-infected patients into two groups. One of these groups wrote about their emotions each day while the other wrote about controlled topics rather than emotions. The researchers concluded, "Based on the self-reports of the value of writing and the preliminary laboratory findings, the results suggest that emotional writing may provide benefit for patients with HIV infection" and also noted that "[t]he results are consistent with those of previous studies using emotional writing in other patient groups." (Petrie) In effect, just writing about feelings seems to improve physical and mental health.

Other studies have used letter writing to help chronically ill patients manage their anger, depression, and pain (Graham), while group painting and music lessons have been shown to reduce depression and feelings of isolation by those with dementia (Hannemann).

A review of scientific studies to explore "the relationship between engagement with the creative arts and health outcomes, specifically the health effects of music engagement, visual arts therapy, movement-based creative expression, and expressive writing" found that "[i]n all 4 areas of creative artistic expression reviewed, there are clear indications that artistic engagement has significantly positive effects on health" (Stuckey and Noble).

In other words, creative pursuits such as listening to music, drawing, dancing, or writing can actually promote good health. And being a manless woman allows you the time to make creative pursuits a priority.

Creativity Can Help Manage Stress and Anxiety

In addition to physical health, creativity can also help with mental health, specifically with managing stress and anxiety. When a person is deeply involved in a creative activity, anxious thoughts fall away. With each stroke of the brush or pen, anxiety lessens, and focus on the activity increases. If painting or writing doesn't appeal to you, consider a passive activity. Studies have shown that listening to music promotes relaxation which in turn decreases stress and anxiety (Krout).

Think about the last time you prepared a meal, read a book, or rearranged your furniture purely for pleasure. Chances are your mind was engaged in the activity at hand rather than on anxious or stressful thoughts. I'm sure you've noticed the adult coloring books which are now plentiful on store shelves. There's a reason for this. Coloring is a creative activity which lessens stress and anxiety.

When you can lessen stress and anxiety, you feel calmer, resulting in a better quality of life and also a better attitude about your life. I once read a story about a woman who woke up feeling anxious and low. She made a list of all the things in her life that weren't working. A few days later, she woke up feeling grateful for her life, so she made a list of the things in her life she felt were wonderful. She compared both lists and the exact same things were on both. If this doesn't speak to the importance of attitude and managing stress, nothing does.

Embark on a creative activity, even if it makes you uncomfortable. Chances are high that any step you take beyond the life you have today will initially make you uncomfortable. Living a manless life is about trying new things and deepening your satisfaction with your life as a result. Sometimes this means you'll feel a little uncomfortable or even self-conscious at the onset. It's OK to feel these things, and once you make a start, you may become so involved in the activity that you won't even remember your discomfort.

Creativity Can Help Solve Problems

Imagine you are solving a crossword puzzle or creating a recipe. While involved in these activities, your mind is learning to consider alternative solutions. Developing this way of thinking via creative activities strengthens your skills in other areas of your life, especially those that require problem solving. Women often juggle many things at once. We may work stressful jobs, raise children, care for aging parents, manage households, volunteer, and participate in community activities. Figuring out how to accomplish all these activities well can be a problem. Though it may seem counterproductive to take time out of our busy schedules to color, cook, or crochet, doing so can actually help us to manage problems throughout the day, which ultimately gives us more time.

It's worth noting that if we approach creative activities with the intention of solving our problems in that specific period, chances are we will be disappointed. It takes time to develop our problem-solving muscles. Though the solution may not come immediately, if we are consistent, we will notice small changes in our problem-solving abilities which will improve the quality of our lives.

Creativity Can Help to Boost Self-Esteem

As we try different creative activities or complete creative projects, we begin to feel better about ourselves. We see concrete evidence that we do, in fact, have talents beyond what we ever thought. Seeing a finished rug hooking on the wall makes a person feel proud of her ability to complete a satisfying project. The new recipe we tried for dinner reminds us that we have the skills needed to satisfy ourselves, while the paint-by-number project hanging in our office shows us we are empowered to create beauty in our lives.

Simply taking a step to try a new activity makes us feel proud of our courage. Whether or not we liked the activity, or were successful at it, is beside the point. This is not about achieving goals nor making perfect products. Nourishing our creativity is about self-discovery and self-growth. There is no end-goal or timeline. The purpose is simply to enjoy the activity without pressure. See where it leads you and learn more about yourself. Do not attach deadlines to these endeavors. Deadlines turn what is intended to be beneficial into work and add unwelcome pressure. Instead, relax, discover, and most of all, have fun.

Creativity Can Help You Express Your Uniqueness

When you are in someone else's home or in another person's car, you can clearly see how unique that individual is. Almost the second you enter someone's living or driving space, you can feel a difference from your own. There are personal items unique to that individual. You may absolutely love some of the things you see, while you may feel reviled by other things. The items may have no association with one other apart from that each item was placed there by the same person. Even in your own home or vehicle, there are likely items that make no sense to anyone but you. This reflects your uniqueness, the individuality that makes you special.

Taking part in creative activities helps you to discover your own uniqueness. Why did you color that flower yellow when another person chose orange? Why is your kitchen painted beige when your friend's is pale green? Why did you add thyme to that recipe when someone else chose garlic? Why is the scarf you're knitting light blue when your friend is crocheting a purple one? Why did you focus on the ocean when you took that photo when the person next to you pointed her camera at the rock to the left?

The answer to all these questions is because you have a unique and special viewpoint that no one else has. By participating in creative activities, you can see concrete expression of your uniqueness. And when you think about the choices you make in these activities, you can also learn a lot about yourself and your preferences. Look at the ways you choose to express your creativity (painting, woodworking, cooking) then consider the choices you make within those activity. What colors are you drawn to? What types of wood do you like? What types of food do you like? Use creative activities as both an expression of your uniqueness and a time of self-discovery. The better you know and understand yourself, the more fulfilling your manless life will be.

Begin With Small Steps

If the idea of being creative doesn't appeal to you, then it may not be right for you. However, before you make that decision, give creativity a try. Start small and see what happens. The best way to begin is to make a list of any type of creative activity you may want to try. If you can't come up with anything, look through the chart below and choose one or two activities that appeal to you.

Woodworking	Cooking	Knitting	Glassblowing
Gardening	Calligraphy	Sewing	Writing Music
Genealogy	Singing	Interior Design	Pottery
Dancing	Drawing	Filmmaking	Scrapbooking
Web Design	Graphic Design	Photography	Painting
Crocheting	Digital Art	Metal Working	Tap Dancing
Creative Writing	Coloring	Playing Guitar	Dog Grooming
Playing Chess	Acting	Blogging	Podcasting
Flower Arranging	Jewelry Making	Balloon Creations	Origami
Soap Making	Doing Puzzles	Journaling	Quilting

Wreath Making	Doodling	Sculpture	Wood Burning
Candle Making	Poetry Writing	Painting Ceramics	Embroidery
Cross Stitch	Making Collages	Painting Dollhouses	Tie Dying
Puppetry	Making Dolls	Flower Pressing	Lego Creations
Making Coasters	Wood Carving	Learning Languages	Paint By Number
Sketching	Making Cards	Building Furniture	Latte Art
Graffiti Art	Glass Blowing	Building Models	Macrame

After you've chosen one or two activities you might like to try, begin by searching online for more information to understand the specifics involved in each activity. Read blogs and online posts about the activity to see if it's something that interests you. If not, try another one. If your interest is sustained, then take the next step toward doing this activity. You can begin some activities almost immediately with little more than a pen and paper. Others require more materials. You may need to find flowers to arrange or press. Painting or knitting will require yarn, easels, brushes, and other supplies. If you're not quite ready to make a financial investment in materials, continue reading about the activity and learning from others who are doing the thing you'd like to do.

Remember, this is not a race. You are not getting graded on it. You do not have to do it perfectly or quickly. You can simply take your time to learn about an activity that you may or may not want to bring into your life. If you decide the activity isn't right for you, sell or donate those materials and move on to another one. If you would like to move forward, think about a way you can do that slowly without pressure. Creative activities are useful in decreasing stress and should not create more anxiety. No goals. No expectations. Take your time and have fun.

Pay Attention to Your Feelings

Try to notice how you feel as you begin your activity. Women are sometimes programmed to do what is expected of them rather than what they actually like to do. It's possible that you may choose a creative activity because you think you "should" select a certain one. If you are unaccustomed to paying attention to yourself, you may not even be aware that you have chosen this activity based on someone else's ideas about your life. That's OK. Let your feelings be your guide. If you absolutely hate what you're doing, stop immediately.

This is not about doing something you "have" to so that you can check off a box. This is about enriching your life and celebrating your manlessness. You should choose a creative activity, in the spirit of excitement and celebration, not in dread. You may feel dread or fear at the idea of starting something new, but if the dread continues while you do the activity, then it may not be the right one for you. Again, that's OK. The entire manless process is about discovering and honoring who you are. Therefore, if something doesn't work for you, you get to let it go and move on.

You Are Worth It

As we near the halfway point of the book, it's worth noting that you may be experiencing many different feelings. Some of you may still feel a sadness from not giving yourself the time and attention you deserved for many years. Others may feel excited and happy about finally being able to nurture themselves and express their creativity. Still others may feel a bit overwhelmed, perhaps even unworthy of all the time and attention they're giving themselves. Children, especially girls, are often told not to be selfish and to think of others and share their time and resources. While sharing is beneficial to a certain extent, they're not applicable to every aspect of our lives. At some point in our lives, we all need to pull back and take care of ourselves.

What most of us are not taught growing up is that taking time for ourselves and nurturing and caring for ourselves makes us happier, more content people in this world. In turn, this leaves us better able to help other people. To be there and help other people, we must first take care of ourselves. The relationship we have with ourselves is the single most important relationship we will have in our lifetimes. It dictates how we will allow others to treat us and how we show up in the world, the ways we deal with successes and challenges, and the amount of happiness we allow into our lives.

If we don't believe we are worthy of time, attention, and caring, then our chances at living a happy, fulfilling life will be limited. We will find or invent reasons to give our time away to other people rather than focusing on ourselves. We will tell ourselves that "little" things such as creativity and self-nurturing don't matter as much as issues in other people's lives. We will procrastinate, never taking even a small step to bring greater fulfillment into our lives, and even more dangerously, we may decide to throw ourselves into an unhealthy relationship to avoid focusing on ourselves.

It Really Is All About You

While we may decide to enter a relationship at some point in our lives, it's important to understand our motivations behind this desire and to consider the relationship's timing. Many newly man-less women, and even some who have been manless for a while, panic at the thought of being "alone" for the rest of their lives. This panic drives them to pursue relationships without ever con-sidering their own needs. I know one woman who, after many decades of being married, joined a dating service before she was even divorced. She conducted an extensive search for the perfect mate, even making lists and conducting "interviews" of potential partners. She found a new relationship before her divorce was even finalized.

There's nothing wrong with wanting to be in a relationship, but it's important to understand your motivation for this kind of con-nection. The woman I mentioned said she didn't want to be alone. Though everyone is different, not wanting to be alone, in my opin-ion, masks a fear of getting to know oneself. It's not always easy to face those people in your life who think you should be married, or at least in a relationship, by now. However, when you understand the value of your manless life and the benefits of taking time to understand your needs, other peoples' opinions of you largely cease to matter. You may even find that their opinions about you are based on their own fears, and never actually had anything to do with you.

This is your time. This is your place. You are manless, and you deserve to be happy. You deserve to take time for yourself. Your needs are worthy of your attention. You get to focus on what you want out of life rather than on what others expect you to have. Do not let anyone else dictate how you live your life. Go out there and find what works for you, and enjoy it!

CHAPTER 6

It's About More Than You

*When you consider things like the stars, our affairs don't
seem to matter very much, do they?*

—Virginia Woolf

As a manless woman, you have more time and energy to develop
your spirituality. For some women, this may involve a traditional
church. For others, spirituality can be a deep realization, or a
sense of something greater than themselves, or a connection to
nature. If you've always been skeptical of organized religion, or if
you don't feel a need for spirituality in your life, try to keep an
open mind. It's possible that your ideas about spirituality are limited. Or, perhaps, you are very clear-minded and still feel there's
no place in your life for a anything similar to spirituality. Whatever beliefs you bring to this book, it's important you make informed
decisions based on your own preferences. No one will force you
to do anything you don't want to do. Still, read this chapter to
decide if anything here works for you in your life.

It's important to be clear on what spirituality is and what it
isn't.

Spirituality is:

- Recognition of something greater than yourself. While this may be labeled as a Great Spirit or a deity, it can also be the flow of the natural world or fate.
- Deeply private and personal.
- A feeling of unity with other living beings. This may come in the form of being part of a group or as experiencing compassion for others.
- Having deep thoughts about the meaning of life, what happens after death, and the purpose of the human condition.
- Great awe or respect for the natural world.
- According to Christina Puchalski, MD, Director of the George Washington Institute for Spirituality and Health, "spirituality is the aspect of humanity that refers to the way individuals seek and express meaning and purpose and the way they experience their connectedness to the moment, to self, to others, to nature, and to the significant or sacred." (Delagran)
- According to Mario Beauregard and Denyse O'Leary, researchers who authored *The Spiritual Brain*, "spirituality means any experience that is thought to bring the experiencer into contact with the divine (in other words, not just any experience that feels meaningful)" (Delagran).
- Nurses Ruth Beckmann Murray and Judith Proctor Zentner write that "the spiritual dimension tries to be in harmony with the universe, and strives for answers about the infinite, and comes into focus when the person faces emotional stress, physical illness, or death" (Delagran).
- According to the Earl E. Bakken Center for Spirituality and Healing at the University of Minnesota, spirituality involves asking larger questions including:
  o Am I a good person?

o What is the meaning of my suffering?

o What is my connection to the world around me?

o Do things happen for a reason?

o How can I live my life in the best way possible? (Delagran)

- In spirituality, the questions are: where do I personally find meaning, connection, and value; while in religion, the questions are: what is true and right? (Delagran)

Spirituality is NOT:

- An affiliation with organized religion such as a church.
- Use of doctrine or religious practices.
- Participation in formalized practices of worship repeated at specific times.
- Reading, devotion, or communal prayer.
- Regular engagement with ancient texts or sacred books.
- Necessarily a belief in a divine being outside of oneself.
- A search for absolution from an authority figure through regular worship or standardized rituals.
- The involvement of intuitions or anointed beings to connect to a religious deity.

Spiritual Activities

Even if you have no interest in developing a spiritual life, you may still want to consider participating in some activities which are spiritually related. You may already be doing some of these things, even if they do not fit with your definition of spirituality. As you continue reading, it's important to keep an open mind and to remember that at its core, spirituality is about connection. Connection with yourself, others, a greater power, and nature (including animals), none of which require a romantic relationship.

Spending Time in Nature

One of the easiest ways to begin taking part in a spiritual activity is to get outside. Spending time in nature provides many people with a peacefulness not easily found elsewhere. Whether it's finding a favorite tree, a patch of sand at the beach, a star in the sky, or a rock in the desert, taking a few minutes to simply observe nature can help you to feel connected to something larger, a grander universe, of which you are a part. Consider for a second how beautiful nature can be. The leaves that turn vivid red or yellow in fall; the vibrantly colored flowers which bloom in summer; the silent, white beauty of snow-covered grass; and the bright-yellow spring sunshine reflected in the deep-blue ocean. These are nature's gifts to all of us.

Also, think about how perfectly every element of nature functions to take care of itself. The Idaho Forest Products Commission says,

Forests are dynamic. While trees go through the natural process of growing—from seed, to seedling, to maturity and eventually death and decomposition—their forest home evolves. Forests move through a predictable cycle and undergo changes that create the conditions for different communities of plants and animals. Each stage of the cycle lays the groundwork for the next.

Taking this a step further, let's include yourself. If a tree has everything it needs to go through its lifecycle, then it stands to reason that you will, too, meaning there's no need to fight against being manless. Simply experience your life as it is today, and work to make it the best possible life for you.

While climate change has put nature in danger, when divorced from human interference, the elements of nature are self-sustaining. Think about yourself in the same way. Spending time in nature reminds us that we are not the center of the universe but only one small part. Our difficulties and challenges are only one small part of our lives and, most importantly, we can and will survive and thrive in the same ways nature does.

Nature's beauty is for all of us to enjoy, free of charge, by simply looking out the window at a tree or the sky. Sunshine can help us remember our own "sunny" side and our potential for great happiness. The clouds in the sky can remind us that our sadness will also pass by, flowing through us, and revealing a bright beautiful blue sky on the other side. Flowers can help us to remember the gifts we have in our lives and can remind us of our roots as we learn to ground ourselves in our own lives. So, find a bench or a rock and sit for a few minutes to enjoy nature's beautiful show!

Yoga

Yoga is another spiritual activity which has received a great deal of attention over the past several years. Yoga has many physical benefits including increased muscle strength, tone, and flexibility, improved balance, pain relief, heart health, increased energy, and the lowering of blood sugar. Yoga also helps with mental health by lowering stress and increasing both mindfulness and sleep quality. In addition to these things, practicing yoga can help you to increase your self-esteem. When you take action to do something healthy for yourself, you feel better about yourself in general. Getting in touch with your body through yoga poses can also give you a new respect for your physical capabilities.

Perhaps one of the most needed benefits of yoga for manless women is a reduction of anxiety. When you are focused on yoga, your mind has little time to conjure up anxious thoughts. Even the most well-adjusted manless woman can't help but feel anxious from time to time when she is overwhelmed with messages about marriage and partnership. Yoga can help to focus your mind on your body to create better health for yourself. If you feel healthy, then you naturally feel better about yourself and your life.

Sometimes beginning something new can feel overwhelming, especially if you've never done anything like it before. It's OK for you to feel overwhelmed. Acknowledge these feelings, then take one small step towards trying the activity anyway. A good first step might be to look at some yoga programs online or find a book about yoga in the library. Take a few minutes to read about the benefits of each move. Then try one of the easy yoga positions to see what it feels like. Don't push yourself to complete an hour-long program the very first day. That's a sure way to put too much pressure on yourself which increases the likelihood that you'll abandon future attempts.

The key is to begin slowly and to continue to move forward in a positive direction. Start with doing one position a few times a week, then add another and another over the weeks that follow. If you're a social person, then you may want to look for a yoga class in your community. Local YMCAs, gyms, senior centers, and adult education services sometimes offer yoga classes. You may even find postings for classes at a natural foods store. If you're not able to find a class that works for you, then invite a friend or family member over as you work through a program together online. It's important to find a method that works for you. If a full yoga course doesn't work for you, then perhaps gentle stretching every day is a better choice. Once again, pay attention to yourself so you can figure out what's right for you.

Meditation

Like yoga, meditation is another spiritual practice which has great benefits. In its simplest form, meditation is to ponder, focus, or concentrate. Not to be confused with thinking, the focus is on the present moment. In many cases, the meditator may focus on their breath or on a specific word called a *mantra*. In some cases, meditating is done by focusing on the pause between inhalation and exhalation, or the abdomen as it rises and falls with each breath, or even a count of in breath and out breath. Other meditation practices involve mindful body scans as a means of relaxing different parts of the body, or a focus on the sound of silence.

According to mindful.org, the five biggest obstacles to meditation are doubt, restlessness, irritation, sleepiness, and wanting. In my practices, doubt is the most powerful of these. When I first started meditating, I did not believe that it would work for me. Even though I saw others benefit from meditation, I did not believe I could or would be one of these people. With continued practice, however, my doubt began to lessen. This did take time. If you, too, are struggling with doubt, mindful.org offers a solution. "We have to remember that thoughts are just thoughts; they're not facts (even the ones that say they are). When we notice this doubt slipping in, just take note of it, perhaps even notice the fear that is often underneath it, and then gently return back to the practice" (Goldstein).

Since the benefits of meditation take time to develop, it can be easy to doubt meditation's effectiveness. This is where the idea of just doing it helps tremendously. It's best not to think about what state of mind we are trying to get from meditation, or how long it will take for us to feel calmer. Instead, focus on being present during the meditation, and let the rest of it take care of itself. Don't plan or plot how long it will take for your anxiety to go away. Don't think about all the things you have to do for the day or where you'd rather be. Just simply focus on the mediation in front of you.

There are many free mediations online and even some paid apps which can help you get started. I use the Calm app and it's helped me to ease slowly into meditation. In this app, there are some programs that are only two or three minutes long and can be done at your work desk during the day. There's also relaxing music and sleep stories, mindful movements, and longer meditation series for specific issues such as anxiety or self-esteem. It's important to remember that what works for me may not work for you. You'll need to be patient with yourself as you try different meditation programs. Be sure to give each program at least a few tries before deciding it's not right for you. As a manless woman, you have the time to explore many different options until you find what works for you.

Time in Solitude

Time alone in solitude is another spiritual activity which you may find useful. Even though as a manless woman, you may have plenty of time by yourself, making a conscious effort to spend time in solitude is different from simply living by yourself. Living by yourself doesn't necessarily mean that you focus on yourself.

Spending time in solitude is a period in which you let your mind wander and learn more about yourself. During this time, you get to know yourself better, and discover more about your likes and dislikes. The more you know yourself, the more you will be able to discover things you like to do. In turn, this will help you to live a more meaningful life and to experience deeper joy.

Your time in solitude should not involve using social media or media of any kind. Put away your phone. Don't compare yourself to anyone else or wonder if you're doing it "right." Instead, think about your life, your goals, or your emotions. Spend time reflecting on the joys and sorrows in your life. Consider creating a plan to manage a difficult situation. Do not, however, spend your time in solitude worrying or trying to change things you can't control. There are many things you can't control in your life, and worrying about them will not help change them. For example, you can't control other people, world affairs, the behavior of others, the choices other people make, or most other things outside of yourself. The one thing you can control is your attitude, behaviors, and choices. Use this time in solitude to understand who you are and what you'd like to bring into your life.

Journal Writing

You may also want to consider writing down your thoughts and feelings during your time in solitude. Journal writing has many benefits including helping you to remain aware of the progress you are making. Writing can help you to notice the changes in your attitudes, behaviors, and ability to process emotions. It can deepen your understanding of yourself, reduce stress, and help you to organize your thoughts. If you journal regularly, you can witness the changes you've made by going back and reading previous entries.

You can also write about strong feelings you are having to release them in a healthy way so you don't take them out on yourself or others. As you write, you will come to develop a better understanding of yourself that will help you to reduce stress and better organize your thoughts.

For me, one of the most helpful aspects of journal writing is an increased ability to clearly understand my feelings about a given situation. I can sometimes have trouble identifying what I'm feeling, but once I start writing, the feelings somehow make sense, and I begin to identify emotions I didn't even know I was having. Taking this further, journal writing provides me with a way to get my feelings out without saying or doing something regrettable. If I am angry, I can write an angry letter to the person I am angry with, which was especially helpful after my divorce. Such letters are never intended to be sent; they are just ways to develop clarity about a situation and to understand whether an issue needs to be further addressed with the other person. By writing, you take the power out of the anger so you can express your feelings in a healthier way that won't destroy a valuable relationship.

As you begin to write, some questions or concerns may come up. You may wonder who you are writing to. For me, I simply write as if I'm writing to a very close friend without any introduction. I do not feel comfortable with the standard "Dear Diary" salutation, but instead jump right into writing. You may also fear that someone else will find and read your journal. If this is the case, then either hide it in a safe place or purchase a lock box or safe. Be aware that people sometimes use this as an excuse not to journal. You are smarter than that. While these concerns are perfectly natural, it you're serious about journal writing, then you need to figure out ways to create a safe writing experience for yourself. You are worth the effort!

Lend a Helping Hand

In addition to connecting with yourself, spirituality is also about connecting with others. One of the most beneficial and personally rewarding ways to do this is to volunteer to help those in need. Being able to aid others spreads kindness throughout the world and helps others to live better lives. Additionally, volunteering of-fers personal benefits to you. Helping others, which includes people and animals, reduces isolation, provides a sense of purpose, improves self-esteem, puts things into perspective, and brightens your mood. Whether this help is in the form of volunteering for an event, helping at a local shelter, or sending a sponsorship check each month, your assistance can help to make life better for both people and animals.

If you're wondering how to get started, the North Carolina Community Action Association lists 45 different ways to help others at their website, some of which include helping a local senior citizen with errands, donating items to food pantries, helping kids learn how to read, mentoring a community member to improve their career, and donating unneeded items to a shelter. If you're better with animals, you can always volunteer to walk or spend time with shelter or rescue animals. I know firsthand how life-changing that can be.

Over a decade ago, I very nervously visited a horse rescue farm for a tour. After that, I began volunteering to help with grooming, walking, and generally socializing horses who had been abused. I didn't grow up with horses, and I knew very little about them. As I mentioned before, I also suffered from balance issues which added to my fears about being around these very large animals. Still, I continued going there at least once a week, and sometimes three or four times per week. Of course, as I'm sure you can guess, I fell in love with a large pony and my entire life changed within a matter of a year. Not only did I meet many wonderful people, but I also ended up adopting three amazing horses who would challenge me in unforeseeable ways and bring more love into my life than I ever imagined.

The pony I fell in love with had been beaten and starved. It took me the better part of a year to get him to fully give his heart to me. He trusted me, not only with his life, but with his heart as well. Each step of the way, I gained his trust. The first time I put a horse jacket on him, he was so afraid, he was shaking. But so was I. Together, we learned how to navigate our fears and live better lives. By the time I said goodbye to him, we had a loving connection like no other. And it was the same with the other two, who I loved just as deeply. Though all three are now in Heaven, my love for horses continues. As I write this, I have two rescue horses who I love dearly. Since I suffer from balance issues, I am unable to ride, so I adopt horses who cannot be ridden any longer. Older horses who can no longer be ridden often experience neglect and abuse. I know that by doing what I can to help these horses, I have changed not only their lives, but mine as well.

This life-changing love began at a time when I was manless and self-pitying, but I made one simple decision: to take a step forward to help neglected and abused horses. Who knows what kind of amazing things you may bring into your life when you begin helping others.

After reading more than half of this book, you've taken in a lot of information. You may be feeling a bit overwhelmed, possibly even afraid of moving forward. Even if the life you've created for yourself may not be the one you want, it is familiar, and making changes and moving forward to create a brand-new life takes courage. You may experience discomfort. You may need to be vulnerable as you learn new things, and most of all, you might have to push aside your fears and insecurities to take a risk. In the next chapter, you'll read more about fear and how to manage it. It's important to remember that as a manless woman, you can do difficult things. And, even if they don't turn out the way you hope, you can try again and again. There is no scorecard here. Each step forward into a new life will lead you in the direction you want to go. So, keep moving!

CHAPTER 7

Face Everything And Regroup

I have learned over the years that when one's mind is made up, this diminishes fear; knowing what must be done does away with fear.

—ROSA PARKS

You've seen it before. A photograph of an older woman on the ground trying desperately to get up with the words, "Help! I've fallen and I can't get up!" This advertisement for a personal notification system is designed to scare not only older people, but also single women. Even though this device can be useful for some who suffer from specific mental or physical deterioration, the underlying message in this ad is that it's not safe for a woman to live by herself; that living alone can result in serious injury. Though this is only one example, there are many other, more subtle media images which depict the single life as being frightening, lonely, and wrong. For example, turn on almost any television show or open almost any magazine and you'll see images of happy couples on vacation, at the beach, spending time with their children, driving brand-new cars, or cooking together. Though these images are not as obvious as the "fallen woman," they are still designed to promote a societal belief that being without a partner is scary and wrong, and that the only way to be happy is to be part of a couple or family.

Fairy Tales

These images aren't just in advertisements. Think for a second about the fairy tales many of us grew up watching and reading. The most obvious example is Cinderella. Consider the message in this fairy tale. Cinderella is miserable until she is "rescued" by a prince. Her stepsisters compete for a man's attention, thus propagating the idea that women must "earn" men's love and be "perfect" to win the "prize" which is a relationship with a man, the only assurance of a happy life. Equally as upsetting is the idea that women must be adversaries if they are to marry and be happy. This is seen in both Cinderella's relationship with her "evil" stepmother as well as with her stepsisters. Competition between women for a man's affection can also be seen in the stepmother's treatment of Cinderella. Though not outwardly spoken, it is clear the stepmother does not like reminders of her husband's past marriage.

While Cinderella is an obvious and much criticized fairy tale, there are many others. There are also some which have been updated to include more empowering representations of women, and yet, the original fairy tales and all their accompanying merchandise continue to survive. Their popularity contributes to disempowering single women. With all the other media available, it may seem foolish to focus on fairy tales. And yet, many experts say a child learns more between birth and age five than at any other time in their life. That is the age when exposure to these fairy tales is at its highest. This means these fairy tales are poised to make a great impact on our lifelong outlook and mindset.

It's easy, and mostly ineffective, to blame one form of media for perpetuating fears about single life when in fact, it's the culmination of decades' worth of antiquated ideas that have created the anti-single atmosphere we now live in. At this point, it's easy to come up with a list of both positive and negative portrayals of single women in the media. However, those that are negative have been around for much longer and are greater in number. Therefore, as manless women, it's important to consider which media messages we allow into our lives. You cannot change the messages that are already out there, but you can "correct" the ideas that have been imparted on you to avoid falling into the fear trap.

"Correct" Media Images

The first step to honestly understanding the image in front of you is to take a deep look at the messages portrayed in the advertisement, television show, or film. The surface message may appear to be one of empowerment, but is that the truth? For example, if you see a single woman, observe how she is portrayed. Do other characters respect or pity her? What setting is she in? Are her belongings and environment upbeat and neat, or depressing and messy? Are there jokes being made about her marital status? Is the portrayal flattering, sexualized, empowering, or diminutive? Does this woman make her own decisions, or is she forced into submission by other characters?

It's important to remember that sometimes what's left out of a media portrayal can be more powerful than what's included. If the program or advertisement you see does not include any portrayals of single women but only those of couples, this also emits a powerful message about unacceptance of single life. If the only single characters are grandparents or older, frail friends and relatives, this, too, promotes a message about manlessness being the result of ageing, rather than a choice made with vitality and excitement.

Next, consider the context in which singleness is portrayed. Is the single person the focus of the advertisement or story, or is he or she in the background? What situation, if any, is faced by the single person? Is this a serious situation, or one in which the single person is mocked or portrayed as inadequate? Is the single person "rescued" by someone else, or empowered to solve his or her own problems?

Now, take a few minutes to decide whether you feel good about this portrayal of singleness. As a manless woman, would you use this portrayal as an empowering example of someone to look up to or emulate? Or do you feel ashamed of being single after watching this portrayal? Sometimes, because of the underlying messages in media portrayals, we may see an image that appears to be positive, yet contains hidden negative messaging. Therefore, it's important to check out how you're feeling. This can help you to better understand the true dynamics of media portrayals.

Finally, as a last step, make "corrections" to this portrayal if needed. If it's a positive and empowering portrayal, then you may want to file it away in your mind for times when you feel less than positive. If, however, it's negative, then the best way to "correct" the portrayal is to provide counter messages. If the image shows a sloppy, mean single woman, then think about a kind, beautiful single woman and remind yourself of her as a way to counter the negative portrayal. If the only happy characters are coupled up, then think about a happy single woman so you can remember that people in relationships are not the only people who are happy.

Attitude is Everything

As you've probably noticed by now, your attitude is the most important determinant of your happiness. If you see yourself as a pathetic victim who needs to be "saved" by a man to make you feel better, then chances are good you will spend much of your life being miserable and desperate. If, however, you consider your manless life to be a blessing, then you will treat it as such and experience deep joy and happiness.

One of the most effective ways to improve your attitude is to make sure you practice healthy lifestyle habits. Overindulging in food or alcohol can lead to depression, while taking on too many stressful activities can lead to feelings of powerlessness. But take care of your body, and your physical health will help lift your attitude. Another attitude booster is to stop criticizing. This pertains to yourself (hopefully you've already begun working with affirmations) and others. It's not up to you to point out everything that's wrong in the world. Instead, why not try to notice how many things are good and right?

One of the easiest ways to improve your attitude is to smile. Smile at yourself in the mirror. Smiling gives you an instant attitude boost and it only takes a second. Taking this a step further, you can decide to practice kindness towards others if that feels right for you. This should be done in a way that makes *you* feel better. Kindness is not only about pleasing others. Being kind and considerate towards others not only makes the world a better place, but it also reminds you of your power to make change, and to be kind to yourself, which is a major mood booster.

You can also boost your mood by taking things less personally. So many of us feel personally offended when someone acts rudely to us or does something we don't like. Even though it seems extremely personal, these actions are about the person doing them;

they're not about us. I remember hearing a story about a man who was on the subway with his two children. His children were young, and they were running around the subway car annoying all the other passengers. Most of the passengers tried to ignore the children, yet they were personally bothered by the kids' disturbance. One kind man greeted the father and mentioned how active his children were. He wasn't mean or judgmental. The man said to him that he and his children just left the hospital where his wife had died. Even though those people on the subway may have thought the children's actions were about them, they were not. Their actions were about what the man and his family were experiencing.

It's difficult for us to understand or know what other people are experiencing at any given point in time. Therefore, it's best to approach everyone with kindness and respect. We don't have to agree with anyone's actions, but we also don't need to be rude or judge them. We can simply acknowledge that other people react to situations based on their own experiences, which have nothing to do with us. By not taking things personally, we can greatly improve our attitude. This is especially true when we sense disapproval or pity from others about our manless lives. Even though it can be challenging, it's important to remember that their attitudes are about them, not us. We do not have to absorb their attitudes, and we need to remind ourselves that no one but us knows what's best for us.

In part, this book is about getting to know ourselves to understand what's best for us, which will give us confidence when faced with criticism or judgment. We don't need to convince anyone that our choices are valid or healthy. We don't have to argue about the benefits of our manless life with others, and we certainly don't need to involve ourselves with other people's ideas of how they think we should live. The bottom line is that our life is our choice. And even though you may be perfectly happy with the life you've created for yourself, sometimes, when faced with criticism or judgment, it's easy to second-guess yourself. The information in this book is designed to help you stay true to yourself and your choices no matter what others say.

Fear of Being Alone

Many newly manless women, as well as those who have been single for a while, find fear of being alone to be their single biggest emotional issue. This fear is strongly perpetuated in society. A recent *New York Times* article outlined the consequences of people living alone, citing, as concerns, issues about housing, health care, and personal finances. (Goldstein and Gebeloff) The article notes that just about 30 percent of all households contain single occupants, with nearly twenty-six million Americans aged fifty and older living alone. Approximately 60 percent of these people are female. Though the article points out that many of these people, when interviewed, said they feel positive about their lives, the "challenges" of living alone and childless are outlined.

In the article, Mary Felder talks about the challenges of living alone and maintaining her Philadelphia row house.

While the *New York Times* is a reputable newspaper, it's important to note that many points of view were left out of this article. The inclusion of one sentence about older Americans feeling positive in their lives does not accurately reflect the large number of Americans who thoroughly enjoy living alone. In other words, there are two sides to this story, yet the article focused on only one. It's also important to note that news outlets generally seek out interview subjects who have a certain point of view. In some cases, they find people who have extreme experiences and opinions to garner attention.

The point, here, is to question the fears highlighted in the article, and to evaluate whether they deserve to be applied to your life. If, for example, you are decades away from being classified as an older American, then this article may be irrelevant to your life. If you are an older American who does not have children, then it may serve you to put a plan together as you age so that you aren't spending your time focusing on fears. Fear is of little use unless we are in eminent danger.

Fear of Being Undesirable

Another fear many manless women face is that of being considered undesirable. In their lowest moments, they may convince themselves that their lack of a mate is "proof" that there is something wrong with them. They begin to think they aren't pretty enough or smart enough. They tell themselves they don't matter. It's understandable that you may have these feelings; I'm quite certain everyone does from time to time. But when they appear, it's crucial you be aware of how false these ideas are. Your worth, or anyone else's for that matter, is not determined by your marital status or what others think of you. Women are manless for all sorts of reasons, some of which include making a conscious choice, while others are due to circumstances such as death, divorce, or lack of suitable partners. None of these are due to the quality of the woman, nor should they ever be viewed that way.

Historically, society perpetuated the idea that some women are not beautiful enough to get married. In years past, some women focused exclusively on their appearance, putting great time into making themselves "worthy" of attention from men as a means of ensuring their very survival. It wasn't until 1920 that women were allowed to vote and 1974 that they were allowed to apply for a mortgage without a male cosigner. Prior to this, most women literally needed men to survive. If they were able to secure jobs, their income was much less than their male counterparts, and their economic challenges were greater. It's important to remember that this is not the case today. Manless women can work high-paying jobs, own their own homes, and live fulfilling lives.

The strong fear of being undesirable or of having something wrong with oneself, is often inherited. Well-meaning grandmothers and mothers who wanted the best for their female loved ones impressed upon them that "snagging" a man meant they would be taken care of and could live economically successful lives. From their points of view, this was the only way a woman could avoid economic challenges. The key here are the words "from their points of view." Women who grew up unable to enter legal contracts without a man, who were not allowed to vote nor have a say in political affairs, and who were seen as being of a weaker sex, can have a difficult time believing or accepting the idea that a woman can be manless and happy. They're viewpoint is certainly understandable; however, it's vital not to let their antiquated attitudes influence your modern life. In other words, don't buy into someone else's ideas about desirability, nor their fears for survival.

Face Your Fears

Before going into ways to manage your fears, it's important to remember that both those in relationships and those who are manless have fear. Fear is not unique to only manless women. The most effective way to deal with any fear you may have about living a manless life is to face your fears directly. Though this may be different for everyone, there are some common actions we can all take to lessen, and even remove, our fears.

Step One: Awareness

To begin, take a few days or weeks to really investigate your fears. Whenever you start feeling afraid, make note of the situation and the way the fear manifests itself. When the phone rings, does your heartbeat quicken? If you're out in a shopping mall alone, do you feel anxious? While lying in bed at night, do you feel afraid? Or is the morning filled with anxiety for you? Do you feel scared attending a social function? Is driving an anxiety-producing event for you?

As you write about these moments, be specific. Were you fearful of the event you attended, or was it the people who were there or the activity involved that produced your nervousness? Did spending money make you anxious, or was it certain stores or the mall itself that caused that reaction? Do the best you can to pinpoint the exact time you began to feel anxious. Do not judge or try to push down your fears. Simply pay attention and make note of as many details as possible. After you've done this for a few days or weeks, go back and review what you've written. At this point, you should have enough information to see patterns. You may be able to identify exactly what your fears are about and when you experience the most fear.

If possible, try to group your fears together. Are there some which directly pertain to being manless, or are most of your fears about other things? Do certain situations cause you anxiety? Are there people in your life whom you fear? Do you experience greater fear in certain settings? Really taking time to review and categorize your fears will tell you much about where your fears come from. Once you have a specific list of your fears and the way they manifest themselves in your life, you can begin to understand where, when, and how your anxiety is influencing your life.

Step Two: Acceptance

Once you've listed and grouped your fears, you'll have a good idea of the things and situations which cause you fear. The next step is to simply acknowledge this new information without judgement or criticism. Do not label yourself "weak" or "stupid" for feeling a certain way. The kindest and most effective action you can take is to accept your fear as part of who you currently are. Being afraid does not make you a bad person. Everyone is scared at one time or another. Fear is a part of life. Though your fears are unique to you, they are not any better or worse than someone else's. Simply look at your list, and tell yourself that you accept your fears as part of your current life.

As you work through the acceptance process, do not try to ignore any of your fears. It's important to pay attention to all of your fears, the ones you understand, and the ones you don't. There may be several fears which don't make sense to you. You may not have any idea why you feel a certain way or where that feeling is coming from. That's OK. Just review your fears and accept that for today, these are the things you're afraid of. These fears may come and go. Some may only be for this minute and never felt again. Whatever fears you have, work to accept them.

Step Three: Investigation

Once you've accepted your fears, it's worthwhile to take some time to investigate where they come from. While it may not be possible to understand the origin of every fear you have, there are many which you can begin to understand. Choose one of the fears on your list which seems to be prominent in your life; the one you experience most often. If there isn't one more prominent fear on your list, then choose whichever you would like to explore.

Now, grab a pen and paper. Take a few deep breaths, and begin to write about this fear. When is the first time you experienced this fear? How old were you? Where were you? Who was with you? Try to include as many details as possible. Let yourself simply write about this fear. If you don't feel comfortable writing, then think or meditate on this fear, focusing on the previous questions. Really think about the different times in your life wherein you've experienced this fear. Does it appear in your life regularly, or is it new? Is it a fear from your childhood which has evolved as you've grown older?

If this activity feels overwhelming to you, you may want to consider contacting a professional counselor for help. Some of our fears can be so deeply upsetting to us that we need help to manage them. There's nothing wrong with that. It takes courage to look at our fears and to learn to deal with them. As we do, the quality of our lives improves greatly.

Step Four: Visualization

Once you've investigated the origin of your fear and filled in as many details surrounding it as possible, you can begin to reframe your reaction to the fear-producing situation. Rather than seeing yourself afraid, begin to visualize yourself feeling powerful and unafraid as you move through the fear-producing situation. Add as many details as you can, and picture yourself unphased by the events. Imagine yourself as unafraid and strong. Focus deeply on how you would move through this situation unafraid. What physical sensations do you experience? Do you feel serene? Calm? Maybe even happy for getting through this without feeling afraid?

For example, if, as a manless woman, you have a fear of getting a flat tire and becoming stranded on the side of the road, you may want to picture yourself either changing the tire, or calling for roadside assistance. If it's opening a pickle jar that concerns you, then take a few minutes to see yourself successfully doing this. Perhaps you'll use a knife to bang on the top to make the jar easier to open, or maybe you'll see yourself grabbing a jar-opening tool for help. Whatever way you handle these situations, picture yourself doing exactly that. Do not fall into the belief that you are not strong enough. Instead, visualize a way to accomplish whatever you need to do.

If you have trouble with visualization, consider putting together a storyboard or drawing a picture of yourself overcoming this fear. For the storyboard, simply draw a few pictures of the activity of you as you progress through your fear. If you'd prefer to draw only one picture, then draw one of you in the final stage of conquering your fear. If you're not comfortable drawing, then find a picture online or in a magazine to represent yourself conquering this fear and imagine how you would feel after moving through it. As with visualization, be sure to include as many details as possible. Where are you? What does the area look like? Can you find a way to express the emotions you feel once you've pushed through this fear?

Step Five: Movement

Once you've gone through the previous four steps, you're likely to experience some leftover feelings. Sometimes, these may be feelings of excitement for having found a way to deal with your fear. Other times, these may be feelings of fear remaining from the visualization. A good way to manage these feelings is to move. Take a walk. Do yoga. Go to the gym. Ride your bike. Play golf. Go for a run. Do something that will help you to release these feelings. If you are unable to move, then take several long, deep breaths or spend some time meditating.

You may also want to consider doing something nice for yourself such as soaking in a warm bath, getting a massage, or watching a favorite movie. Learning to manage fear isn't always easy, but the freedom it provides is worth it.

Manless Life Fears

Though the method outlined previously can help you manage your general fears, there are several additional fears that are specific to living a manless life. The two biggest, fear of being alone and fear of being undesirable, have already been discussed, however, there are others which have a more practical nature to them. These are fears about daily living, and can include finances, health, safety, home maintenance and repairs, and other such considerations.

As Bella DePaulo, author of *How We Live Now: Redefining Home and Family in the 21st Century*, noted in a recent *Atlantic* article, cost savings on bulk items may not be something those living alone can take advantage of since food products are often perishable. She also notes that recipes are portioned for families, and single people are sometimes expected to work longer hours since they don't have a spouse or children to care for. As noted in the article,

> Some aspects of travel, particularly lodging, are much more expensive, per person, for single people. These all may seem like small annoyances, but in practice they are regular reminders that American society still assumes that the default adult has a partner and that the default household contains multiple people. More concerning, some health-care protocols are essentially built on the assumption that a patient lives with someone who can support them (Pinsker).

It's all too easy for manless women who live alone to develop fears around these things. While the process outlined in this chapter can help you to deal with these fears, a more practical approach may be necessary.

Financial Fears

If you're concerned about your finances, it's important to proactively develop a plan to address your fears. Make a list of your expenses. Track your spending. Create a budget. Learn to live within your means. Sell items you no longer need. Plan a yard sale if that works better for you. Buy items in bulk when possible. If you're having trouble, consult an expert for help. Look for one through a nonprofit organization or an employee assistance program or find a book to help you.

Though it certainly is understandable for manless women to have financial fears, it is possible to lessen, if not eradicate, these fears through action. Take full advantage of any retirement benefits offered by your workplace. Put money into savings each month even if it's a small amount. Pay off high-interest credit card debt. Buy only those things you can truly afford. Learn to recognize the difference between wanting something and needing something. You may want a brand-new SUV, yet one that's several years older can get you where you need to go just as reliably, all while saving you thousands of dollars.

An important part of any financial plan includes savings. Though it can be easy to bypass this practice, do not fall into that trap. Having a savings account, and contributing to it regularly, is one of the easiest ways to manage anxiety about finances. It's simply a part of life that things will need repair at some point or another. With a savings account in place, you have peace of mind to know you can afford to fix what's broken without stress or worry.

Health Fears

Fears about getting sick or having an accident when living alone can be very powerful. There are ways you can help to lessen these fears. To begin, if you feel as if you're getting sick, you may want to stock up on food and medicine. Ask someone to check up on you, even with simple phone calls. Even if you aren't feeling sick, it's a good idea to keep necessities in your home. The next time you cook a meal, freeze some, so you'll have it the next time you don't feel well. Keep a supply of easy-to-prepare foods in your pantry, and first aid and over-the-counter medicines in your bathroom cabinet.

If you're especially concerned about your health, you may want to arrange a daily check-in with a friend or family member. Perhaps this person contacts you at the same time each day. This can be as simple as a morning or evening text, or as elaborate as a daily visit. Whatever you choose, be sure you're comfortable with the situation to prevent this contact from becoming a burden.

If you need to have a medical procedure which requires someone else to drive you to or from the hospital, and you do not feel comfortable having a friend or family member take you, consider hiring a driver or setting up a barter system with a neighbor. Perhaps your neighbor can drive you to the appointment, and you can help your neighbor with something else. It's also worth investigating any transportation services offered in your community. Social media is another good resource. Many towns and cities have Facebook pages designed to provide information about resources to residents.

Safety Fears

Many living alone have fears about safety, which include falling. If you are at an age where this is a concern, or if you have medical issues which make this a reality, then you may want to consider an app or emergency notification system. You could also make a concerted effort to always keep your cell phone nearby. Take a few minutes to go through your home and remove any items you might trip over such as area rugs with upturned edges. Be sure to keep floors dry to avoid slipping on wet spots.

If you have fears about the security of your home, you may want to consider checking the locks to make sure they are secure, or installing an alarm system or additional locks on windows and doors. If something is weighing heavily on your mind about your security, take steps to remedy the situation. Feeling safe in your home will go a long way in alleviating fears you have about security.

Fears About Home Maintenance/Repairs

Many manless women are fearful about home maintenance and repairs. One way to manage these fears is to begin educating yourself about how various things in your home operate. You do not need to become an expert on every aspect of your house; instead, strive to develop a basic knowledge about how to manage your home. For example, learn how to shut off the main water valve in case there's a plumbing leak. Figure out how to turn off the furnace in the event of an emergency. Know where the main electrical shut off is, and how to restart a breaker if it's flipped.

If the thought of learning these things overwhelms you, take a deep breath and consider an attitude change. Think of yourself as an explorer going on a quest. Take it one appliance at a time. Grab the instruction manual or, if you don't have it, look online and learn the basics of how that appliance operates. If you have a dishwasher and it has a filter, learn how to change it. If your stove has a pilot light, become familiar with how to light it in the event of a power outage. Rather than feeling defeated and overwhelmed, work to develop a "can do" attitude. Grab a screwdriver, buy a drill, and get started!

Another important tool in your toolbox is to create a network of professionals who can help you. Most likely, there will be some repairs and tasks that you won't be able to complete. For these, you'll need to hire professionals. Ask neighbors and friends. Go online and do research. Consider purchasing service contracts for appliances such as your furnace if they're available. These cover you for certain types of repairs. If finances are an issue, consider a barter system with friends or neighbors. I know a woman who cooked dinner for her friend, and in exchange, her friend cleaned her furnace. The arrangement worked well for both.

Fear of What Other People Think

A chapter about fears would not be complete without discussing the fear of what other people might think. As a manless woman, this fear can sometimes feel overwhelming. Some women feel as if everyone is looking at them when they attend an event alone or go out by themselves. Others simply refuse to attend events without a friend while still more avoid social functions all together. If you have no interest in attending events, then by all means, excuse yourself. If, however, you decline invitations due to your manless status, take a few minutes to consider several things.

Most People Don't Care About What You Do

Though it may sound harsh, the fact is most people are not scrutinizing your life in the way you think they are. Most people are thinking about their lives and their needs, not yours. They are most likely not, as you imagine, watching your every move and criticizing it. Instead, they are doing exactly what you are, scrutinizing themselves and wondering what others are thinking of them. This is true of most people, regardless of their relationship status. No one is immune to feeling insecure. Manless women often feel insecure in specific social situations.

Consider, for a second, attending a wedding by yourself. Does the mere thought of this make you uncomfortable? Can you already feel the anxiety creeping in? Well, take a deep breath and think about this. If this is a wedding you really want to attend, then go, have fun, and do your best not to think about what others are thinking about you. Instead, enjoy the ceremony, the people, and the dancing if that's your thing. However, if you are attending this wedding to "show" everyone how OK you are with your manless status, or if you are going because you feel as if you must, reconsider whether you need to be there. By its very nature, a wedding is a celebration of a committed relationship. As a manless woman, you have decided not to be part of a relationship. The two don't seem to go together, and beyond that, trying to prove something to someone else usually backfires and results in painful feelings.

This is not to say that you should never attend another wedding. Instead, it is to encourage you to consider whether you truly want to go to this wedding. Think about your own beliefs. What are your thoughts about marriage? Do you believe in the concept or not? Would you like to be there to see these two people commit to each other, or would you prefer not to be part of that? These are questions only you can answer, and the answers need to come from your own values and beliefs. Attending an event because you "must" is not a good reason. It's easy to convince yourself that your friend or family member needs you there, but is that assessment actually true? If it is true, should his or her needs come before your own? If, on the hand, you really want to attend, then try to come up with a plan to make it more enjoyable for you. Can you skip the reception but go to the wedding? Or would you rather do the opposite? The important thing is to construct a plan that works for you.

Everyone Has an Opinion

Of course, other people will have all sorts of opinions about you and your life. Some of them may even express these opinions repeatedly. The trick here is to accept that other people have their own opinions, but that their opinions are their business, and you don't need to live your life according to them. It is impossible for anyone who is not you to have enough understanding of you to know what's right for you better than you do. You are the one who knows what's best for you, and if you don't know that, then take some time to figure it out. Relying on other people's opinions to measure how well you're doing in your life is a setup for frustration, and it will result in an unfulfilling life for yourself. It's also worth considering why you believe someone else's opinion of you is more important than your own. What qualifies this person's opinion to be so important?

It's natural to want people to like you but putting their opinions before your own causes two major problems. The first is that we put this person on a pedestal, looking up to them for approval which can result in deep disappointment. No one is perfect. When we make a person in our life so important that their ideas about our lives matter more than our own, we have created a situation which has the potential to cause resentments against this person, and deep feelings of inferiority within ourselves. By looking to others for approval, we are telling ourselves that our opinions don't matter, or are less important than those of the person we have put on a pedestal.

The second of these problems is that putting other people's opinions before our own means we never really get to know ourselves and our likes and dislikes. Instead, we are working so hard to live according to this other person's opinion, that we shut the door on ourselves. And should we lose contact with this person, we are left feeling lost since we never took the time to get to know ourselves. This type of situation can result in great sadness, depression, and feelings of abandonment, first by this other person, then by ourselves.

Mindreading

It's also important to remember that you are not a mind reader. You truly don't know what someone else is thinking unless they tell you, and even then, you have only their word. It is not possible for you to be inside of someone's mind to know exactly what they are thinking. Read that sentence again. It is not possible for you to be inside of someone's mind to know exactly what they are thinking. All too often, we think we know what someone else is thinking when we don't. More times than not, we are much harsher with ourselves than anyone else ever would be with us. We have blind spots about ourselves, and in many cases, these blind spots are about our attributes. In other words, we are harder on ourselves than anyone else, and we all but ignore our own positive qualities. This is the perspective from which we are "reading" someone else's mind.

Simply put, even if we think we know what someone else is thinking, we absolutely do not. In fact, we don't even know if they're thinking about us. That scowl on her face may be reflecting her stomachache, not the outfit you chose. The angry look may have nothing to do with you. Other people's lives are about them, not you. You are not the focus of their lives, and if you are, then you may want to reconsider having them in your life.

The Source

Whenever you begin to worry about what other people are thinking of you, consider who it is that you're actually worrying about. Is this person a stranger on the street? A friend of a friend? A family member? And why is this person's opinion of you so important to you? Why do you care what this person thinks of you? How will their opinion affect your life? Will it really matter? What thoughts are you afraid they're having?

Examining the source will help you get to the bottom of your fear about what others think of you. If you tend to worry about what everyone thinks of you, you can talk yourself out of this fear by reminding yourself that most of these people matter little in your life. If, however, your fear involves a close friend or family member, then you may need to look a little deeper. Think your fear through. What are you worried will happen if this person thinks poorly of you? Are you afraid of losing a friendship or family relationship? If so, try to imagine your life without this person. Chances are, though you may not choose this outcome, your life would be OK without this person in it. If you feel that it wouldn't, then begin to work towards giving yourself some of the time and attention you give this other person to lessen his or her hold over you.

It's worth noting that the fears mentioned in this chapter are not unique to manless women. Married women and those in relationships have many, if not all, of the fears listed here. Not only is being afraid a universal condition for both women and men, but it's also perpetuated in many aspects of our society. Think for a minute about some of the advertisements you've seen. Many encourage you to *act now* so you don't miss out on a deal. These try to scare you into purchasing products that you may or may not need. Experts estimate we see between three-to-five thousand advertisements every day, a significant portion of which expose us to fear.

Being in a relationship would not take away your fears. In some instances, it's just the opposite. If you have a deep fear of being undesirable, a relationship may highlight and even increase this fear. It's unrealistic and unfair to think another person can magically take away all your fears. Consider what a burden it is to the other person when you make them responsible for how you feel. Since they are not able to change how you feel, chances are you will both end up frustrated and angry with each other. Your anger will come from the unrealistic expectations you've put on another person to "fix" you, and their anger will stem from being unable to give you what you want, and resenting the position you've put them in.

Please take a few minutes to get that message deep into your head. No one else can "fix" you or "save" you. No one else can stop you from feeling something you don't want to feel. You are solely responsible for your life and your feelings. This is the single most important thing for you to remember throughout this book.

As you move through your manless life, you may experience other fears. It's important to remember that fears aren't facts. Believing your own interpretations can sometimes cause more problems than the actual event. So, if you feel afraid, begin with three deep breaths, then put on your thinking cap and figure out how to deal with your fears. You can do it!

CHAPTER 8

All Creatures Big and Small

I think having an animal in your life makes you a better human.

—RACHEL RAY

They're cute. They're furry. They're fun to watch. And most of all, they can turn a house into a home. Many manless women choose to welcome pets into their homes. Not only do these furry creatures provide abundant affection, but they also help to alleviate loneliness and offer a wonderful outlet for compassionship. Before you run off to adopt a pet, be sure to read this chapter to make sure you find the right pet for you. Animals, like people, have an enormous variety of characteristics, and not all pets are right for every person. Having a pet at all may not be right for you. If the thought of caring for anything other than yourself overwhelms you, then move on to the next chapter. There are far too many animals in shelters because someone didn't take time to consider the responsibilities of pet ownership. If you are interested in welcoming a pet into your household, then continue reading. To find a pet that works with your lifestyle, you may need to consider different types of animals.

Species

When you think about a pet, do you imagine going on long walks with a dog, snuggling up with a cat, listening to a bird sing, watching a fish swim through the water, or riding a horse? Would you prefer to spend time with a rabbit, a gerbil, a guinea pig, chickens, ducks, or even a snake? Or are you fascinated by goats, donkeys, or lamas? Take a few minutes to think about what type of pet you're looking for. If, for example, you aren't particularly fond of the outdoors, then caring for animals that live outside or need to be taken out regularly may not work for you. If you spend very little time in your home and are often outdoors, then you may want to consider a species who lives outside the house.

If you're drawn to one species over another, do some research to understand what's involved in the care of that animal. It's worth getting in touch with an organization or person who is familiar with the habits of the species. If possible, spend time with these animals before adopting one. Volunteer at a shelter. Just be careful to remain as objective as possible. Do not fall for a "pretty face" when that type of pet may not be right for you. Try to pay attention to the care of the animal and not its cuteness. This is easier said than done, but remember, you can always make a donation if you'd like to help a particular animal.

If you'd like to adopt a pet you've never had before, you may want to consider finding a local rescue to see if they offer a sponsorship program. This will allow you to help an animal and become familiar its needs prior to ownership. Before I adopted my three horses, I spent six months volunteering at H.O.R.S.E. of Connecticut, a local rescue for abused and neglected horses. The organization offers educational seminars and hands-on experience with horses, which prepared me to care for these amazing animals. This time as a volunteer helped me to become familiar with many different horses until I found the ones who were right for me.

Time

How much time do you have to care for a pet? If your first response is *none*, then move onto the next chapter. All pets require some amount of time, even those that seem low maintenance. In addition to spending time feeding and cleaning up after them, you will also need to shop for their food and provide them with an adequate living environment. Take time to think about the care necessary for each species. A fish, for example, may not require as much time as a dog, yet the fish still needs its water changed and regular feedings.

Be aware of the misconceptions about animals and time. Many think cats don't require much time. While they may not demand as much of your attention as dogs, they do need to be fed, petted, played with, and cleaned up after. If you're looking for an "easy" animal, you may want to consider whether you have time for a pet. One of the biggest reasons animals end up in shelters is because the person who adopted them does not have the time to care for them. If you're unsure, it's better to wait. This will avoid traumatizing an innocent animal. Wanting a pet doesn't mean you have the time to care for one. As a manless woman, you need to be sure you can afford to care for a pet, and that your lifestyle will support the choice of pet ownership. For example, if you have a passion for travel, then having a pet may not be right for you. Perhaps volunteering several times each month is a better option for you.

If you find that you don't have enough time to care for the pet you'd like, then you may want to volunteer or pet sit instead. This will give you the ability to spend time with an animal when it works for you, rather than devoting hours each day to care for one of your own. If you do have the time and are interested in adopting a companion, then be sure to think about how you can adjust your schedule to care for your new pet. If you work outside the home eight or more hours a day and you are interested in having a dog, you may need to plan to have someone come in and walk or feed the dog during that time.

Activity Level

You'll also need to consider how active you'd like your pet to be. A puppy or a kitten will be quite active and may require you to chase after them. In the case of the puppy, you'll also need to walk him or her. Different breeds have different energy levels. A border collie will have more energy than a shih tzu while a Maine coon cat will have less energy than a Burmese cat. Older dogs and cats won't be as active, though they will still need attention. If you're very active and love to spend time outdoors, you may consider larger animals who require a great deal of work. If you like to spend time watching television, then a sedentary animal may be better for you.

If you've decided on a specific species, think about how the activity level of that species matches your own. Adopting a young horse who needs to be ridden three or four times a week may not work for someone who isn't physically fit. However, there are plenty of older horses who enjoy taking a walk a few times a week. When you have decided on a species, try to figure out a way to make it work for both of you. In the horse example, if you don't have a large enough yard, you can board your horse. Or you can lease or sponsor a horse, which would allow you to spend time riding or walking the horse yet not actually being completely responsible for it.

If you have children, be sure to take them into account when considering different species, but do not rely on your child to care for your pet. Too many pets are abandoned when a child grows up and his or her parent can no longer care for that pet. Be sure to choose a pet whose activity level works for you at this point in your life. An older cat who likes to snuggle but not move around too much would not be a good match for a household with an active toddler. That house may want to consider a young-adult pet with a good disposition.

Age

The age of any pet you select matters greatly when determining if that pet will fit with your abilities and resources. Younger animals will need to be trained and perhaps even socialized, while many older animals are all set. As with people, animals age in very different ways. Though you may want to do some research on the lifespan of the pet you are considering, keep in mind that these numbers are simply an average of how long the animal may live. Even animals with the same parents can live varied amounts of time.

I had five bunnies who were from the same litter. The average lifespan of their breed is six to nine years. Four of the bunnies died right around six years, while one is still going strong at over seven. Another litter was born a month later, and of those, four are still living while only one passed away year six. All these bunnies had the same mother and father and were born within a month of each other.

Also, some pets live very long lives. An African Grey Parrot can live thirty to fifty years. Horses can live twenty to thirty years or longer. Umbrella Cockatoos can live seventy to eighty years. Goldfish can live for ten years, and indoor cats can easily live ten to fifteen years or more. Chihuahuas can live up to twenty years. Hamsters have an average lifespan of only two or three years. Guinea pigs generally live between four and five years, while gerbils average three or four years.

As you can see, there are vast age differences between different species. It's important to consider not only the age of the animal, but also your own age, to be sure the animal is cared for throughout its entire life. If you're planning to adopt a younger animal who may outlive you, be sure to make arrangements for that animal should you pass.

Finances

Different species of pets require different financial commitments. The cost to care for a horse can be upwards of $4,000 per year and, in some cases, more than double that. According to Money Management International, care for a dog can cost between $700 and $2,000 per year, while care for rabbits and cats costs roughly $500 and $1,100 per year. The cost for guinea pigs is between $500 and $800 per year. Hamsters and small mammals will set you back between $300 and $500 per year (Campbell).

When considering the cost of care, also think about vet bills. Surprisingly, gerbils topped *USA Today's* list of most expensive pets at the vet with owners reporting spends of over $500 per visit. Mice, alpacas, goats, and chinchillas rounded out the top five, according to the article (Craven).

Your Needs

Perhaps one of the most important things to consider when getting a pet is your needs and what you'd like from a pet. Are you looking for companionship at home? A pet to travel with? A working animal who will provide wool, rides, or eggs? A protector or an animal to show? Think about what you'd like a pet to bring into your life. One of my very best friends has a golden retriever who competes in dock-diving contests. This activity not only allows a young, energetic dog an outlet for his energy, but it's also an activity they do together, and it allows her to socialize with other dog owners.

It's tempting to ignore your own needs when you're looking into the eyes of an animal who needs a home. But while we all want to help animals in need, this scenario is dangerous for both you and the animal. Adopting an animal who does not meet your needs will only cause frustration for both of you and may result in a failed adoption. Ultimately, this will cause more harm to the animal than if it had remained at the shelter. To prevent this, pull out your journal and make a list of the things you'd like to do with your pet should you decide to adopt one. If you'd prefer to do nothing with your pet but watch it, that's valuable information too. Some people find great serenity in watching fish swim in their tanks while others love to observe their guinea pigs as they hold them.

If you are seriously considering welcoming a pet into your life, the single most important thing you can do to ensure a successful adoption is to be clear on what you need and want from that pet. Remember, women are often told to put aside their needs for the greater good of others. While this may be necessary in some cases, in the situation of pet adoption, it will only cause harm. If you truly get attached to an animal who is not right for you, then sponsor the animal first. If that goes well, perhaps you can foster the animal to be sure it works with your needs. If you adopt an animal who is not right for you, you will end up resentful and bitter. That is not what a manless life is about. A manless life is about doing what works best for you in as many different areas of your life as possible.

Adoption Alternatives

If, after reading the information in this chapter, you're still not sure adopting a pet is right for you, then you may want to consider alternative ways to bring animals into your life. You could:

- Volunteer at a local shelter. You can usually find a list of shelters online or from national organizations such as the American Society for the Prevention of Cruelty to Animals (ASPCA).
- Sponsor an animal. Many organizations offer sponsorship programs where you pay a certain amount each month to help care for an animal of your choice. Some even encourage visitation with that animal. H.O.R.S.E. of Connecticut offers a sponsorship program in which you donate $50 a month to support a rescue horse. As part of this program, you can visit with "your" horse once a month.
- Foster a pet. If you're not ready to make a long-term commitment to an animal, then consider "borrowing" an animal from a local rescue. As part of most foster programs, you provide a safe place for the animal to live until it gets adopted.
- Get a job working with animals. If you're considering a career change or just want to pick up a part-time job, you may want to think about working with animals. Vet's offices, boarding

facilities, shelters, and even some rescue organizations employ people to care for their resident pets.

- Pet sit for friends or family members. Offer to take care of your friend or family member's pet when they are away on vacation. This will allow you to have some time with a furry friend without adopting a pet of your own. As a bonus, your friend or family member will be grateful to leave their precious baby with someone they trust.
- Volunteer with animal conservation organizations in other states or countries. If you can't take on a domestic pet right now, you may be able to help make life better for animals in the wild. Start with either the US Fish and Wildlife Service or the World Wildlife Fund to find volunteer opportunities both in the United States and other countries.
- Attend pet shows. Many local and national organizations sponsor pet shows. For dog shows, start with the American Kennel Club. For cat shows, it's the Cat Fanciers' Association and for rabbits, the American Rabbit Breeders Association.
- Follow a shelter blog or sanctuary online. Many rescue organizations and animal sanctuaries post regular updates and even videos about their residents. Some of the most popular YouTube bloggers include The Humane Society of the United States, Big Cat Rescue, Friends for Life Animal Shelter, and Angels Among Us Pet Rescue.

Be Sure

No matter what decision you make about having or not having a pet in your life, take time to be as certain as you can be. If you are in doubt, then wait a little while until the decision is clearer to you. This is especially true if you are newly manless and trying to fill a void in your life. Take some time to understand your new lifestyle before rushing into anything. If you have decided to welcome a furry friend into your life, then I wish you both all the best and hope you will be happy together. I know, firsthand, the amazing joy that pets can bring into our lives.

Read on and discover how to make an even bigger choice about your manless life in the next chapter.

CHAPTER 9

Choices, Chances, and a Higher Plan

Most of us become more conscientious, confident, caring,
and calm with life experience.

—ANGELA DUCKWORTH

If you've completed even a small portion of the suggested activities in this book thus far, you've developed a greater understanding of yourself and your values. You've learned more about your preferences, and most importantly, you've made choices based on those preferences. This might be the first time in your life that you've paid such attention to yourself. Or, being with yourself again may feel like a homecoming. There's still so much more to discover as life moves on.

Though it's impossible to know what will happen in the future, we can make the best of today and pay attention to the choices we make, to have fulfilling, happy, lives. For those who are newly manless, making choices based on our own needs and preferences might be a brand-new experience. For those who have been manless for a while, there is some familiarity to the process. In either situation, the absolute "secret" to a happy life, if there is such a thing, is to make decisions based on our "real self" rather than on the opinions of society or other people.

Finding Your "Real Self"

When we talk about our "real self" we can relate this directly to Thomas Merton's three-stage process of understanding the true self, which involves understanding the self, understanding God (or whatever deity you worship), and understanding others. According to Merton, this process will ultimately result in compassion towards others. If you want to develop your spirituality on a deeper level, Merton's process can be a valuable and enlightening journey. Regardless of whether you want to develop your spirituality, it's important to develop an understanding of your needs and how your "real self" is manifested in your life.

Those who do not take time to understand themselves often repeat the same unhealthy and even dangerous patterns throughout their lives. As manless women, this could mean becoming involved in unhealthy relationships, whether with friends or romantic partners. It might also mean choosing a place to live that doesn't meet your needs, working at a job that you don't like, spending time with people you don't relate to, or even choosing a hobby you find boring. In other words, discovering your "real self" in whatever way works for you is the foundation of making choices that support your preferences.

While it's not necessary to adopt Merton's deep contemplative approach, some contemplation about yourself is important to develop an understanding of your "authentic self." All the suggestions in this book are geared toward the goal of helping you to get to know yourself, the real you, not the one society tells you to be. So, if you've skipped over some of the suggestions, you may want to go back through the previous chapters and revisit them. If you've done many of the suggested activities and would still like to develop a deeper understanding of yourself, then keep reading for additional suggestions.

Start With Quiet

In today's media-saturated world, it is often hard to hear yourself think. With our phones constantly at the ready, televisions blaring, and music filling the air, there is very little, if any, silence in our lives. In our homes, we may hear traffic or neighborhood noises. In our cars, our favorite songs or talk programs take us away from ourselves. At work, we may hear coworkers, machines, or music throughout the day. There are few, if any, places where silence is the norm. Though you don't need to go away for a silent retreat, taking time to sit in silence, wherever you can find it, is a valuable tool in getting to know yourself.

Be aware that at first, it may feel very uncomfortable to experience silence. There is an adjustment period, and you may need to begin slowly. Start by shutting off all noise for one full minute, then work your way up to more. During this time, think about your life. What's working? What would you like to change? Do not make this a gripe session about your circumstances, but instead, an honest inventory of your life. Do not spend the time criticizing yourself, either. This is not helpful, nor will it assist you in getting to know yourself better. Instead, think of one thing in your life that you are happy with. What about this thing makes you happy? Why do you like it? After that, try to think about two or three more things that you like, and ask yourself the same questions. You may begin to see a pattern. For example, if the things you like are objects, are they all the same color? If the positives in your life are people, do they have similar characteristics? If the things you are happy with are events, do they all evoke similar feelings in you? Whatever emerges for you, don't judge it. Just take note of the similarities, then keep building on them to discover more about yourself.

Take An Inventory

In your times of silence, you will begin to see assets and even a few deficits which are present in your life. Some of these things may be personal life situations (having a wonderful family or losing a friendship; having a healthy body or getting older; experiencing financial success or enduring a stressful work situation) while others may involve societal circumstances (economic outlook, political climate, or social welfare). Either way, think about the times in your life when you have felt most alive, then consider the following questions. What were you doing? Who were you with? What emotions do you feel? Now, do this for the times in your life when you feel unhappy or angry. What are you doing? Who are you with? What emotions do you feel?

Try to do this for at least three or four activities in your life. You can consider events from years ago, but try to look at recent events as well. As you write your answers, include as many details as you can. This will help you to become clear about those things in your life that bring you joy or unhappiness. Remember, you should not be writing negative things about yourself. The purpose of this inventory is to discover the *situational* assets and deficits in your life. You are not uncovering personal assets and deficits. This inventory is about discovering those events or activities which make you feel happy, and those that don't.

It's also important to note that you are not required to change any of the circumstances you discover while taking this inventory.

In other words, don't put pressure on yourself to make drastic changes to your life immediately. Instead, simply create an awareness of the things in your life which bring you happiness. You may decide to bring more of these things into your life, or you may not. There is no pressure to act at this point. Simply pay attention to your life and your circumstances. Though you may choose to make changes, do so when it feels right to you; don't rush just because you wrote something down.

Discover Who You Are

After you've finished your inventory, review it closely. Begin to understand who you are, not who you've always wanted to be. Understand exactly where you are right now, and consider how many things in your life make you happy. It may help to journal about what is working. Do not write about the things you want to bring into your life or that you'd always like to have. That's not the purpose of this activity. The purpose is to discover who you are at this minute in time. This doesn't mean you can't make changes eventually. However, to make sustainable changes, you must first understand who you are.

Remember, you are writing about what's working in your life. You are not writing about all the things that are wrong with you or with your life. That is not the purpose of this activity. It's better to begin with the things that are working. If your first reaction is that nothing is working in your life, take a deep breath and reconsider. Think about all areas of your life, which include your living situation, your friends, family members, work, hobbies, pets, health, or recreational activities. Begin with basic, smaller elements in your life. If, for example, your living situation isn't ideal, do you have a favorite spot or a favorite item which is working?

Is there a particular family member to whom you feel close? A friend you know will be there for you no matter what? Look at each area of your life and make a list of those things which bring you happiness.

After you've done this, and only after, should you begin to consider the things in your life which are not working. In this case, you should list both specific and general things such as a specific outfit you don't like or a hobby you've grown bored with. It's not necessary to list every aspect of the hobby if you generally don't like it anymore. The idea, here, is to get some information about areas in your life that you can make some changes or adjustments to if you so desire. Perhaps that hobby you are bored with can be expanded into one which brings you deep enjoyment again.

As you are making your lists, think about who you are and what makes you *you*. There are certain characteristics, likes, dislikes and facets of your life that make you who you are. No one else in the world contains these exact same qualities. While, of course, you can find many people who you have things in common with, there is no one person who is exactly like you. That alone should tell you how very special you are. It should also tell you that your uniqueness needs to be honored and not pushed into a box created by society. As Frank Bruni points out in a recent *New York Times* editorial, "in an era that exhorts everyone to respect the full range of human identity and expression, there can still be a whiff of stigma to living uncoupled in a household of one." Living a manless life is a way to honor your uniqueness.

Recognize External Influences

This stigma, as Bruni notes, is further illustrated by the fact that 'Spinster' applies to an older [single] woman; for an older

[single] man, there's no term with the same cruelness and cur-
rency." When working to find your real self, it's important to
put aside external influences and ideas. Outright rejection of the
term spinster is a good way to begin. Make a choice to leave this
word completely out of your vocabulary. Do not allow others to
use this word in your presence, and do not read or listen to anything that reinforces this idea. Consciously decide to reject all
external influences regarding this word and society's sometimes
degrading view of singlehood.

Instead, focus deeply on yourself and your attitudes. How do
you truly feel about being single? Do you enjoy being able to make
decisions about your life without considering anyone else? Are
you happy with your life the way it is? Can you find fulfillment in
the activities which make up your life? Is there a serenity to your
life that you enjoy? Are you able to live each day with a reason-
able amount of enthusiasm?

Really think about these questions. How many are you able to
answer *yes* to? For how many was your response negative? It's
worth noting that having a relationship will most likely not change
any of these answers. Though you may initially have the "glow"
that comes from the excitement of a new relationship, a relationship cannot and will not provide personal fulfillment in all areas
of your life nor will it fix all the problems you may be experiencing. A relationship is a way of connecting with another person; it
is not a means of fixing your life.

To get a true picture of your life and discover who you really
are, take a few days to go on a "media diet." Stop watching television. Stay off the internet and social media. Don't read the
newspapers. Put down the romance novels and magazines. Turn
off the radio. Instead, spend time in a place you love (unless, of
course, this a movie theater) and consider what it is about this
area that makes you happy. If you're outdoors, what about being

there do you like? Are you drawn to trees, leaves, bodies of water, the sky, clouds? Try to break it down as much as possible to allow yourself to fine-tune the things you are interested in.

When you return from your "media diet," be conscious of what messaging may be influencing your attitudes and behaviors. For example, when you see a commercial for a new makeup product, do you believe you have to copy the way the model looks? If you see a friend on social media with a new hairstyle, do you begin to think about changing your style as well? Do you spend too much time looking at fashion websites to "perfect" your look? If you walk by a boutique, do you feel you need to buy the outfit?

These are only a few of the ways in which we let external influences change who we truly are. The world in general, and the advertising industry specifically, work hard to make us believe we need to buy or own certain products to make us look or behave in specific ways, even if these ways go against who we really are. Consider the small business owner, the vegan, or the homeschooling parent. Think about the minimalist or the nondrinker or the nonmedia user. All of these lifestyle choices are in direct violation of socially accepted norms. The same is true for being manless in a society that reveres coupledom.

When we allow social norms, the media, or anyone else to influence our lifestyle choices, we accept a set of rules and guidelines which have nothing to do with who we authentically are. Instead, we have chosen a socially acceptable way of living; one which keeps us in a safe little box free from the criticism that may come with making choices outside those norms. And while following social norms may seem easier in the short term, in the long term, all creativity, uniqueness, and passion will be driven out of our lives because we'll have chased a false acceptance born of being like everyone else. Social norms prevent honest, true evaluation of individual preferences. Being manless is a courageous choice that goes against these norms.

Step Back

After you've completed some of the previous activities, take a step back. Put your journals aside and stop thinking about your true self for a while. Try to take a few days, or even a week or two, away. Live your life, and be gentle with yourself. Take a bath if that's something you like to do. Sit in a comfy chair by the fire and read. Watch your favorite television program. Take a long walk or drive. Go to the beach. Have coffee with friends. Relax. Breathe deeply. Whatever it is that makes you feel nurtured, do it.

Taking a step away from self-reflection can help you to return with a fresh perspective and new insights about your life. More than that, it will also give you time to relax and enjoy life. Taking a break can prevent fatigue, increase creativity, and restore focus. It can also allow you time to connect with friends and family members and to rest and recharge.

Making Decisions

After taking some time away, you'll be in a better position to make decisions based on your own preferences. If you've taken time to complete some of the activities throughout the book, you will also have developed a deeper self-awareness which will guide you in making good decisions for you. A good decision is one that takes into consideration the best outcome for you, and if applicable, others involved. Following are some suggestions to help guide you in the process of making good decisions.

Identify the Decision

Though this may seem very basic, the foundation of all good decisions is the identification of the actual decision being made, and not those things related to it. For example, even though you've aways wanted to live in a certain country, the actual decision might really be about where you work rather than where you live, or it may be the opposite one, where you live if you're willing to take any type of job. Identifying the exact nature of the decision is an important first step. Consider if there's a problem that needs to be solved (whether to take a vacation) or a goal to achieve (relaxing), and which of these is the truer decision.

When considering any situation, you need to start by figuring out what the most important decision is that you need to make. This will be the primary decision that drives the smaller ones. In the "where to vacation" situation, if your need to relax is the main decision, the place to vacation will be secondary. Even though the two decisions may go hand in hand, you may find a situation wherein the perfect vacation takes place in spot and the perfect place to relax exists in another. Being clear on which one is the primary decision (in this case, relaxing) will help you to decide between the two options.

Having clarity about the decision you need to make also enables you to understand all the different aspects of the choices available to you as well as the varied paths you can take. From this clarity, you will also be able to more effectively complete the remaining steps outlined.

Collect Information

The next step in making a good decision involves collecting necessary information and weighing the pros and cons of your options.

A good first step is to conduct an online search regarding the choices you have available. In the work example, this would mean looking at websites from different companies you would like to work for, or it could involve researching different career options within a certain company. As part of this process, you may also decide to reach out to others who work in the field or for that particular company. It may help to read professional publications about the company or career you've chosen.

Some of the information you collect will come from yourself, your preferences, and perhaps even some of the activities you've completed in this book. Weighing information includes considering your own needs and thinking about what will make you happy and what will leave you feeling good about your choices. It's also a good idea to think about all the possible consequences of each decision. For example, if you decide to take a job that involves traveling, a consequence of this means you will not spend as much time in an office or at your home. On the other hand, if you take a job in which you spend eight hours every day in an office, then perhaps you won't be able to have a pet, or you'll need to ask for help in caring for it during the day.

Collecting information and making a list of all the possible outcomes of each decision helps you to develop clarity about how this decision will affect you and your life. It's normal that you may begin to imagine worse-case scenarios. Add them to the list. Doing so may help you understand all aspects of the outcomes you are considering. A word of caution here. Don't let this list develop into a means of frightening yourself out of making decisions. Listing the worst-case scenarios is a means of creating insight; it is not an invitation to worry. Worrying does not solve anything, and it may lead to paralysis and missed opportunities. Simply make yourself aware of all the consequences of your decision without focusing on any one result.

Evaluate the Evidence

Taking the information you've collected, think about each alternative. What would they be like? How would you feel if you chose one option over another? Think about each option from beginning to end. See it all the way through. If you decide to find a job as a web developer, consider how you will spend your time during the day. What would your office look like, or would you work from home? How would your time be spent each day? What types of websites would you be developing? Who are the people and companies you would be working for and with? If you decide to work in human resources, think about the protocals you will implement and the interactions you'll have each day. What type of company will you be working for, and who are the people you will be interacting with daily?

While you're evaluating the evidence, it's a good time to notice any incongruities with your personality. If, for example, you are a people person, chances are that staring at a computer screen for eight hours each day may not work for you. If, however, you are an introvert, then working in human resources probably isn't the best career choice for you. At this stage, be sure to draw on those personality traits and preferences which are your own, and not those someone else labeled you as. Many times, as you begin to consider different scenarios, your body will guide you in making the choice that's right for you. If your stomach aches every time you think about speaking in front of people, or if you feel nauseous at the thought of sitting in front of a computer all day, your choice will become clearer to you.

As always, paying attention to yourself is critical. If you don't have physical symptoms, then think about emotional ones. Do you feel overwhelmed thinking about preparing a presentation or working on a website? Are you anxious about working with people or technology? Does it scare you to think about organizing large amounts of data? Noticing your feelings is one of the most important steps in evaluating the choices before you.

Decide

There will come a time to make a decision, to choose a path or course of action. In some cases, you may not have a strong preference for either path. Then, you'll need to select whichever option is slightly more appealing to you. In some cases, you will feel strongly led toward one alternative or the other. Neither situation is wrong or bad, nor should you put pressure on yourself to make a "perfect" decision. There are few, if any, things in life which are perfect. Expecting perfection from yourself in your decision-making process is a way to put unnecessary pressure and stress on yourself. There are no perfect decisions. Though some decisions may result in positive outcomes, it's important to remember that we will not be able to see the consequences of the decisions we make until we are living with them. Sometimes a decision we thought would give us a positive outcome doesn't, while something we were sure was "bad" brings a positive change to our life.

Rather than spend too much time overthinking each decision, do your best to choose the path which seems right for you today, based on where you are in your life at this moment. It's just not possible to know how you will feel days, months, or years down the road. Over time, your likes and dislikes may change. You may find yourself interested in things you never thought you would be, or you may experience life-changing events which alter your perspective. There simply is no way to plan for everything that will happen in our lives. This is why it's important to do the best we can now.

Review the Decision

After you've made your decision, live with it for several days, a week, a month, or even a year, then take some time to review the decision. Is it working for you? Are you happy with the outcome? Was this the best decision you could have made? Would the alternatives have worked better for you? Do you need to adjust anything to make your decision work better in your life? Do you need to make a different decision?

As you ask yourself these questions, and understand it's OK to change your mind. Making a different decision or changing your mind does not label you "weak" or "bad." It simply makes you a person who changed her mind. There is absolutely no shame in changing your mind just as there's nothing wrong with sticking to a decision you made even if others don't agree with it. Living your life in a way that works for you is not about pleasing other people nor living up to societal expectations. It's about paying attention to who you are and honoring your life.

Manless Forever?

At some point in your life, you may choose to make a different decision about your manless status. Once again, there is no right or wrong path here. You may decide, as my eighty-nine-year-old grandmother did, to remain manless for the rest of your life, or you may choose to become involved in a romantic relationship. Unlike years past, many women now consider their marital status to be fluid, moving with the flow of their lives as they grow into different stages. As manless women, we are very much aware that we don't need a man to take care of us or to make our lives complete. Our very survival does not depend on being married or having a man in our lives. With this knowledge comes a freedom to decide how we want to live our lives.

Making a decision about whether or not to remain manless may take some time, or it may happen quickly. If you use the decision-making process outlined earlier in this chapter, you will have a good foundation with which to make this choice.

Lifestyle

If you've lived a manless life for a while, consider the lifestyle you've enjoyed. Up to this point, you've had the freedom to do what you want and to keep your living space as you'd like. Entering a relationship will, most likely, involve compromises about your lifestyle, even if they are small ones. For example, when you welcome someone else into your life, you may need to adjust the temperature in your home, the volume of your music, or the neatness of your space.

Whatever your decision, it's important to make sure it comes from what you want in your life, and not from other people's ideas about what your life should be like. Do not decide to date to keep someone in your life quiet about your lifestyle choices or to please someone else. Instead, decide based solely on how you want to live your life. Since so many of the messages in society tell us how wonderful it is to be in a relationship, it can be easy to underestimate the beauty of your manless time. Understand how many freedoms you enjoy as a manless woman, then think about how these freedoms can remain in your life even if you decide to become part of a couple.

Clarity

If you do decide to date or become involved in a relationship, it's important to be aware of what your intentions are as. Do you want to keep it casual and meet lots of new people, or would you like to be part of a committed relationship? The answer to this question should come from your own ideas about what you'd like in your life. If you're not sure about the answer, then it may not be the right time for you to date.

It's also important not to become focused on this one area of your life. You may decide not to decide, meaning you will let things happen naturally and will resist making any decisions unless you are faced with a dating invitation. As a manless woman, you have learned how to take care of yourself, how to focus on your needs, and how to meet your own needs. Even if you choose to date again, your focus needs to remain on your life and what works for you. Having been brought up in a society which celebrates coupledom, it's all too easy to start imagining "happily-ever-after" coupled endings. It's important to take a more realistic approach to dating.

There is no one person who will make your life perfect. You will not find a "Mr. Right" who will solve all your problems and make your life worth living. Being in a relationship does not mean you will no longer feel lonely or sad. In fact, if you are in an unhealthy relationship, you will feel even lonelier than you would if you were single. This is why having clarity about your own needs will help you to find a fulfilling life.

Another component of clarity is to understand what worked and what didn't work in past relationships. If you are considering dating, it will be important for you to be aware of possible destructive behaviors and patterns that were present in your last relationship. Though it may be easy to blame the other person, that doesn't help you to develop healthy new habits. Instead, consider what in your own behavior worked, and what didn't. Think about the times you were unhappy and the reasons you felt that way. Was there truly inconsiderate behaviors, or were your expectations too high? This is not about vilifying anyone (including yourself). It's about looking for areas you can improve to make your dating experiences more fulfilling for you.

Individuality

Before dating, consider the individuality you have enjoyed as a manless woman. You can, and should, preserve this individuality in a relationship. Doing so will take effort on your part, and if you haven't had enough time to celebrate your own uniqueness, you can easily become buried under the glow of a new relationship. If you're accustomed to pleasing other people, it's possible you may let your individuality slip away through a series of small choices that don't support who you are. You may, for example, decide to attend an event with your date even though you'd much rather be at home. A few days later, you may order the same meal as your date even though you really wanted something else to eat. A little while later, you might decide to skip your weekly family dinner to be with your date. Later that week, perhaps you cancel plans with your friends to spend more time with your date. You may even call in sick to work the next day to have additional time together.

Though we may all do one or even a few of these things on occasion and there may be nothing wrong with that, it's important to be aware of your actions. In the previous example, within the course of a few weeks, you've given up home time, food you like, family time, friends, and work. All these things are important areas of your life that make you unique and contribute to your individuality. Giving them up can be cause for concern. It's possible that you may be falling into the idea of looking to a relationship to make your life happy. As you know, the only one who makes your life happy and fulfilling is you.

Being in a relationship does not necessarily mean you must give up your individuality, however, in many cases, you may need to make compromises about how you spend your time. As you are making decisions about your future, it's important to be aware of these compromises. If, for example, you want to live your life exactly as you prefer without making any compromises, then perhaps you should not begin dating or trying to be in a relationship. Maybe you never will want coupledom. That's OK. Knowing who you are and what you want out of life is the very best way to experience joy and happiness.

Your Decision

Only you can decide what a fulfilling life looks like to you. If you've completed many of the activities in this book, you have a better idea of who you are and what you enjoy. If you haven't, I urge you to go back through and complete at least a few of the activities in each chapter. Though, as a society, we teach many things in schools, we do not educate children or adults in how to learn about themselves. We do not encourage individuals to pay attention to their own needs, nor to follow their own path if that path veers from societal norms. In most cases, we are taught to conform to societal rules, expecations, and behaviors, which include getting married and having children. In some countries, women are not allowed to attend schools or make any choices related to their lives. In other countries, pressure to conform is more subtle, with images of women being wives and mothers fill the airwaves in the form of advertisements, television shows, and movies. The messages in both cultures are the same: a woman's life is not complete without a husband and children.

How you live your life should reflect who you are, not what you've been told you should be. Having had some manless time already, you are closer than others to figuring out your preferences and needs. Since you've read this book, you are also aware of the many societal forces that work to force you into a certain "box" designed to dull your individuality. You're also aware of the fact that you do not need to listen to these forces, nor do you have to please anyone else. Your life choices are your own. You make your life happy and complete. If your life is not happy or complete, getting into a relationship will not make it so. It is, and it has always been, up to you to make your life wonderful and joyous.

In the final chapter, you will learn how to help spread the word about the joys of a manless life, and how to assist other women who are just beginning their manless journeys. Though you cannot take away the challenges someone must go through, you can share your experience and strength to help other women.

CHAPTER 10

Spread the Word

There are two ways of spreading light: to be the candle or the mirror that reflects it.

—EDITH WHARTON

I have the perfect guy for you.
Are you dating anyone?
You'll meet someone when you least expect it.
Have you tired online dating?

We've all heard these things and many of us know firsthand how extremely hurtful they can be. While we can't stop others from saying these things to us, we can decide not to say them to other manless women. Instead, as Edith Wharton notes, we can be a "candle or the mirror that reflects it" by refusing to make our, or other women's marital status, the focus of conversations or get-togethers. Instead, we can come together as women to support other women.

This is not to say that we should never talk about relationship issues when our friends come to us for support. It does mean not focusing on anyone else's relationship status nor constantly asking how they are doing in a pitying way. Even as manless women, it's easy to fall into the societal patterns about relationships when talking with friends.

Pay Attention to Your Words

The first step in supporting other manless women is to pay attention to what you are saying to your friends and those around you. While you may know better than to ask pointed questions about your friends' love lives, you could be contributing to a climate of preconceived notions about how women should act, or even more harmfully, you could be creating a competitive environment with other women. Women have been encouraged to compete with each other for the attention of men. Consider beauty pageants, for example. Women compete against each other so a panel of mostly male judges can determine which woman is most beautiful.

Think about how many movies, books, websites, television shows, and magazine articles portray or instruct women in how to "get" a man. A quick online search results in hundreds of thousands of websites promising to instruct women in how to get a man. One of these even promises tricks on how to get him to marry you. Some promise "practical ways" on how to make a man fall in love with you or to get him to commit, while others include entire books on the subject. Now, add to this the stereotypical portrayals of women in advertisements. A recent ad for a popular cleaning product released around Mother's Day encouraged women to "get back to the job that really matters" indicating that women should be responsible for household cleaning and childcare.

Every time we, as women, accept these stereotypes, whether they be about a woman's "place" in the world or her marital status, we contribute to harming and degrading other women. If we, as manless women, become aware of the words we speak and reject outdated, sexist images of women, we can begin to create a more accepting environment for all women, which will in turn provide a foundation for true acceptance of manless women.

Listen More Than You Speak

One of the most effective ways to support other manless women is to simply listen when they want to talk. This means really listening and not sitting there thinking about what to say next. It does not mean turning the conversation around to focus on yourself but genuinely, truly listening to the woman in front of you. Don't try to fix her problems. Just simply listen. In our fast-paced world, the skill of listening to each other is one for which we are not trained. Quite the opposite, we are trained to ignore robocalls, advertisements, and many other annoying things. Lost in all of this is our ability to listen to others. Following are some suggestions on how to improve your listening skills.

- Make eye contact. Look directly into your friend's eyes. Do not look at your phone. Do not look off into the distance. Look into her eyes. Many of us minimize the importance of this crucial step in the listening process. Not only does eye contact make a person feel heard, but it also helps you to listen better.

- Minimize both internal and external distractions. A noisy room is not a good place to have a heart-to-heart. Neither is lunchtime if you're already starving. If an intense disagreement with someone has left you feeling distracted, take a few minutes to center yourself so you can again be in the moment.

- Don't interrupt. Even if you feel as if the person is taking too long to get to the point of her story, sit there and listen. Wait. Don't rush her through it. Everyone is different. People approach conversations in very different ways. Some need to provide a lot of background information while others get straight to the point. When you interrupt someone, not only are you interfering with their internal process of expressing themselves, but you are also giving them the idea that what you have to say is more important than what they are talking about.

- Suspend all judgments. If you're sitting there judging what your friend is saying, you are not listening. Stop all judgments. Do not assume you understand the person's point of view until she has finished speaking. You may be surprised by what she says, and even if you're not, at least you'll be clear about the point she is making.

- Don't give advice unless you are asked to, and even then, think twice about it. It's so tempting to think we know what's best for someone else when, in reality, we can never be sure. Each person is different, and they come to this life with different thoughts and feelings. We can never really know what someone else feels, which means we can never be sure what they should do. Giving advice oftentimes makes us look like know-it-alls who think they are better than others. Genuinely listening without offering advice provides a safe, supportive environment for our friends to share their feelings without judgments.

- Monitor your body language. If you're sitting there with your arms crossed over your chest, you are sending a subtle message that you are closed off from the conversation. Instead, if it seems appropriate, you may want to nod encouragingly as your friend speaks. In some cases, this may not work. It will be up to you to choose the appropriate body language for the conversation.

Organize Manless Events

One of the best ways to support other manless women is to organize a manless event. Some women, especially those who are newly manless, may be looking for friends and activities. As a manless women, you can guide them in living a fulfilling life. Begin by inviting a few friends over and ask them to bring a friend who is manless. Select a theme or activity for the event and have fun! Following are some ideas for manless nights.

- Spa Night: Have everyone bring a favorite nail polish and face mask then take turns helping each other to feel glamorous!
- Game Night: Grab a few of your favorite games and get everyone playing!
- Clothes Swap Night: Do you have a beautiful blouse that just doesn't look right on you? Gather up all the clothes you don't wear anymore and ask everyone else to do the same then take turns going through each other's bags. If your friends are different sizes, then you can make this a Clothes Donation Night where everyone gathers clothes to donate to charities.
- Vision Board Night: Have everyone bring some old magazines, glue, and scissors along with a posterboard then get busy putting together a vision for the next year of your life. After you're done, be sure to invite everyone to talk about their goals.
- Craft Night: Choose a craft or have everyone bring something to work on and have fun! You may choose one craft for

everyone, such as knitting or sewing, or have everyone do something different. You may also want to consider working on a project to donate to a charity such as a blanket or sweater.

- Movie Night: Get everyone together to watch the newest movie. You can go out to the cinema or stay in and stream!
- Tea Party: Buy some gourmet tea and add a few sweet treats to organize a good old fashioned tea party!
- Yoga Night: Download a yoga program and stretch out those stiff muscles together!
- Book Club Night: Have everyone read the same book and get together to talk about it. Many books have questions included at the end to keep the conversation going.
- Cooking Night: Find a favorite recipe and get cooking together!
- Learn A New Thing Night: Want to learn self-defense? Wood working? Knitting? Dancing? Tarot card reading? Origami? Painting? Whatever it is, ask everyone to chip in and hire an expert to broaden your horizons.

Even though most suggestions listed here involve stay-at-home activities, you may want to organize an out-of-the-house manless event for you and your friends. Here are some ideas of things to do:

- Check out the newest exhibit at a local museum.
- Go to the zoo.
- Visit a spa or mineral spring if there's one nearby.
- Play miniature golf, go bowling, or try tennis.
- Take an adult education class together.
- See a show. This can be from the local high school or all the way up to Broadway.
- Pick berries or pumpkins or even a Christmas tree.

- Try karaoke.
- Go to a flea market or craft fair.
- Take a hike at a local park.
- Attend a concert.
- Go to a lecture.
- Take sailing lessons or learn to drive a speedboat.
- Try skydiving if that's your thing.
- Go dancing or roller skating or, if it's cold, ice skating.
- Try horseback riding.

Whatever activity you decide, whether it's at home or out somewhere, the most important thing is to choose a group activity which will connect other manless women. Women sometimes take their friends for granted or neglect them, putting all their emphasis on a romantic relationship or on their children. Many newly manless women find themselves with few, if any, friends who have the time or interest to participate in activities outside of their families. These women may not be disinterested in spending time with other women; they're simply maxed out from the busyness of managing family activities and work lives.

When planning a manless activity, remember that you won't be able to please everyone, and maybe not even most people. Find something you're interested in, and invite others to join you. If it goes well, all the better. If it doesn't, that's OK too. You can try again with a different activity. Organizing events is another way to explore your likes and dislikes, and you may discover an activity which turns into a passion.

After the event is over, pay attention to your feelings about the event. Did you enjoy spending time with the people who attended? How did you feel about the activity you organized? What worked well and what needed a little improvement? How could you improve the event? Did everyone have enough time to complete the activity? Would you prefer to try a different type of event (in-home rather than out of the home or vice versa)? Are there other women who you may want to invite to future events? Is there someone who didn't seem to enjoy herself?

By asking yourself these questions and reviewing the event in your mind or on paper, you can explore ways to make future events even more fun for you and other manless women. If the event wasn't exactly how you wanted it to be, don't give up! Try again! It will be worth it to know you've helped other manless women.

Make Changes to Support Manless Women

Support businesses and organizations which highlight manless women and their lifestyles. While we can do this on a grand scale by refusing to buy products or services or frequent businesses who practice stereotyping in their advertisements or protocols, it's also possible to make small changes in our everyday lives to recognize manless women. Following are some suggestions.

If you are responsible for making policies at your workplace, build flexibility into the schedule. Manless women (and many who are not manless as well) oftentimes have difficulty scheduling repairs during work hours or attending children's school activities. Allow for flex and work-at-home time when necessary.

If you work in customer service, consider the words you use. As a manless women, I have regularly been addressed as "Mrs." even by those who claim to be inclusive. Do not automatically assume that every woman you encounter is married or has children. The safest salutation is Ms., which is a neutral alternative for Miss and Mrs. or the newly introduced, gender-neutral *Mx.*

- If you are able, mentor other women in your workplace. Many manless women need mentors at work as well as in their personal lives.
- Stop criticizing manless women. There is often a stigma attached to being single in communities where most people are married. Sometimes, people will search for the "flaw" that made a woman manless, which often results in criticism or judgment. Decide not to participate in this practice, and instead, look for what's good in each person you meet.
- Become a manless cheerleader. Make a conscious effort to offer encouragement to manless women whether it's at work or in your daily life. Take a few seconds to offer a compliment for good work. It may be just what that woman needs to keep her moving forward.
- Challenge the idea of bossy women. In general, when a woman is assertive, she risks being called "bossy," while men are seen as confident. Stop buying into this idea. Women do not always have to be sweet and likeable. Women are not bossy nor inconsiderate just because they set boundaries and ask for what they want.
- Support businesses run by manless women. While it may be challenging to identify these organizations, if you do know a manless woman in your community who runs a business, go out of your way to support it.
- Avoid buying products whose advertisements include stereotypical images of married women, while avoiding portrayals of manless women.
- Whenever possible, buy products from businesses who support women in general and manless women specifically.

Of course, it may not be possible to do all these things but the important thing is to make an effort in your daily life to support other manless women. Not only will this help to lessen the societal stigma associated with manlessness, but it will also slowly promote acceptance.

Consider for a few minutes how powerful it would be if every woman across the world took only one action to help manless women every week. The changes this would bring about are mind blowing. Imagine a world where manless women are given the same respect and consideration as married women. Think about what an amazing place the world would be if we stopped considering marriage and motherhood to be a woman's greatest accomplishment.

Final Thoughts

This book is filled with suggestions and ideas about how to create a fulfilling manless life for yourself. And though you may drift from a manless life to a married one or something in between, the importance of taking responsibility for your own life cannot, and should not, be underestimated. It is no one's job to "fix" things in your life, and if you do decide to enter a relationship "broken," then chances are pretty good that your relationship will be unfulfilling. Too many times, I've seen women twist themselves into pretzels trying to please men. Whether they do this to "get" a man, "keep" a man, or marry a man, the result is usually an unhappy relationship based on untruths. Many times, the women in this situation find themselves committed to someone they have little in common with because the relationship was based on "pretend" things she led him to believe were true.

If you're reading this book to make yourself "good" enough for a relationship, then you've missed the entire point. You are already good enough, and a relationship is not some endgame to seek out and pursue. Instead, pursue your own happiness and ful-fillment without worrying if you will ever find someone. Consider yourself the single most important thing in your life. Do not allow others' thoughts or suggestions to influence what you know is true for you. Be strong and believe that a manless life is worth living. Find others who support you in whatever choices you make, and most of all, believe in yourself.

Believing in yourself doesn't mean you will always make a decision that feels right for you. You're human, and just like everyone else, you will make mistakes. It is from these mistakes that you will learn and grown. You will understand who you are and what makes you happy without letting outside forces influence you. To do this, you may need to take a break from social media, and perhaps, media in general. Both are saturated with unrealistic images of happy relationships and families. If you find yourself looking longingly at images of relationships and families, think about that longing.

Do you want to compromise how you spend your time? Do you want to make sacrifices in the things you like to do? Would you feel comfortable living with another person? Do you want to consider another person when making decisions? Consider the things in your life you would have to give up. Though it's a nice notion to believe that you can "have it all" in a relationship, it's not realistic. With only twenty-four hours in a day, chances are that you will need to give up certain activities to find time to spend with your significant other. Of course, it's possible to have a healthy give-and-take that involves mutual compromise. That's the goal of any relationship. However, many women take it upon themselves to be the ones who sacrifice their time and activities.

Most women have been raised to be caretakers, which makes it even more difficult for them to recognize the sacrifices they are making to be in relationships. A good rule is that both people in a relationship should be making compromises to spend time together. If only one person is, then the relationship may not be mutual. In the same way that manless women need to pay attention to themselves, they also need to carefully consider whether being in a relationship will work for them.

Deciding to Stay Manless

There are many women who make a conscious choice to stay manless for their entire lifetimes. Some of these women want to devote their time and attention to their careers. Others are women who have been married and divorced and are done with relationships. Still others have been widowed, and choose not to enter another partnership. Many women stay manless due to life circumstances. Whatever the reason, if this is your choice, then it's important for you to honor it and approach your life in a way that makes you happy.

Begin your new manless life with a commitment to yourself. Decide to support yourself in following your dreams, honoring your life, and loving yourself above any other person in the world. This does not mean you are selfish, but self-caring, which is very different. You are more able to provide love and support to your friends and family if you care for yourself than you can if you neglect your own needs. You are the most important person in your life, and your actions should reflect this. You deserve to be happy, and now is the time for you to take steps to make that happen.

This doesn't mean you should expect instant happiness because you've decided to live a manless life. Quite the opposite, true happiness comes from taking daily steps in the direction of whichever goals are most important to you. There is no magic bullet in a manless nor married life. Both require commitment and dedication, yet in very different ways. In a manless life, your commitment is to yourself and your happiness, while in a married life it is to the partnership. Neither is right or wrong, better or worse. As with most things, it's about what works best for you.

Works Cited

Bruni, Frank. "I Live Alone. Really, I'm Not That Pathetic." *The New York Times*, 9 Dec. 2022. (https://www.nytimes.com/2022/12/09/opinion/living-alone-single.html).

Campbell, Jesse. "Average Annual Costs of Popular Pets." *Money* Management.org, 6 July 2022. (https://www.moneymanagement.org/blog/ranking-your-favorite-pets-in-order-of-cost)

Craven, Scott. "Kids Want A Critter? See Which Pets Are The Most Expensive at The Vet." *USA Today*, 7 Aug. 2017. (https://www.usatoday.com/story/life/allthemoms/2017/08/07/most-expensive-pets-america-vet-bills/34911585/).

Delegran, Louise. "What Is Spirituality?" *University of Minnesota Taking Charge Of Your Health and Well Being*, 2023 (https://www.takingcharge.csh.umn.edu/what-spirituality).

Gardener, Juliet. "The Story Of Women in the 1950s." History Today.com, 9 Sept. 2015 (https://www.historytoday.com/reviews/story-women-1950s).

Graham, J.E., M. Lobel., P. Glass. *et al*. *Effects of* Written Anger Expression in Chronic Pain Patients: Making Meaning from Pain. *J Behav Med* 31, 201–212 (2008). https://doi.org/10.1007/s10865-008-9149-4

Goldstein, Dana, and Gebeloff, Robert. "As Gen X and Boomers Age, They Confront Living Alone." *The New York Times*, 1 December 2022. (https://www.nytimes.com/2022/11/27/us/living-alone-aging.html?smid=url-share).

Goldstein, Elisha. "Overcome These Five Obstacles to Your Mindfulness Practice." Mindful.org, 19 Aug. 2019 (https://www.mindful.org/overcome-these-five-obstacles-to-your-mindfulness-meditation-practice/).

Hannemann, Beat Ted. "Creativity with Dementia Patients. Can Creativity and Art Stimulate Dementia Patients Positively?" *Gerontology vol. 52,1 (2006): 59-65. doi:* 10.1159/000089827

Idaho Forest Products Commission. "As Trees Grow, Forests Evolve." 2023. (https://www.idahoforests.org/content-item/tree-forest-life-cycle/).

Krout, Robert E. "Music Listening to Facilitate Relaxation and Promote Wellness: Integrated Aspects of Our Neurophysiological Responses to Music." *The Arts in Psychotherapy*, vol. 34, 2 (2007): 134-141. https://doi.org/10.1016/j.aip.2006.11.001.

North Carolina Community Action Association. "45 Creative
    Ways to Help Your Community." NCCAA, 2 February
    2021. (https://www.nccaa.net/
    post/45-creative-ways-to-help-your-community).

Petrie, Keith J, et al. "Effect of Written Emotional Expression on
    Immune Function in Patients with Human Immunodeficiency
    Virus Infection: A Randomized Trial." *Psychosomatic
    Medicine vol. 66,2 (2004): 272-5. doi: 10.1097/01.*
    psy.0000116782.49850.d3

Pinsker, Joe. "The Hidden Costs of Living Alone." *The Atlantic*,
    20 Oct. 2021. (https://www.theatlantic.com/family/
    archive/2021/10/living-alone-couple-partner-single/620434/).

Stuckey, Heather L, and Jeremy Nobel. "The Connection
    Between Art, Healing, and Public Health: A Review of
    Current Literature." *American Journal of Public Health vol.
    100,2 (2010): 254-63. doi: 10.2105/AJPH.2008.156497*

Wells, Eleanore. "Why I Said Yes to Staying Single." *Woman's*
    Day.com, 30 Sept. 2011 (https://www.womansday.com/
    relationships/dating-marriage/a5967/
    why-i-said-yes-to-staying-single-124127/).

The author of six popular books, a freelance writer for over 30 years, an associate professor of Communication Studies at Sacred Heart University in Fairfield, Connecticut, a former contributing writer for Fairfield County Home magazine, and a nationally renowned weight-loss expert, Debbie Danowski, Ph.D. has made a career out of educating people about personal growth.

Most recently, Dr. Danowski, who is a recognized academic expert in the public relations/advertising and journalism fields, has been teaching a Studies in Self-Help class at Sacred Heart University for five years.